Practicing Persuasive Written and Oral Advocacy

Case File II

Practicing Persuasive Written and Oral Advocacy

Case File II

David W. Miller
Professor of Law
University of the Pacific
McGeorge School of Law

Michael Vitiello
Professor of Law
University of the Pacific
McGeorge School of Law

Michael R. Fontham
Adjunct Professor of Law
Tulane University Law School
Partner, Stone, Pigman, Walther, Wittmann & Hutchinson

ASPEN
PUBLISHERS

1185 Avenue of the Americas, New York, NY 10036
www.aspenpublishers.com

Printed in the United States of America.

1 2 3 4 5 6 7 8 9 0

ISBN 0-7355-3644-9

ISSN 1539-4603

About Aspen Publishers

Aspen Publishers, headquartered in New York City, is a leading information provider for attorneys, business professionals, and law students. Written by preeminent authorities, our products consist of analytical and practical information covering both U.S. and international topics. We publish in the full range of formats, including updated manuals, books, periodicals, CDs, and online products.

Our proprietary content is complemented by 2,500 legal databases, containing over 11 million documents, available through our Loislaw division. Aspen Publishers also offers a wide range of topical legal and business databases linked to Loislaw's primary material. Our mission is to provide accurate, timely, and authoritative content in easily accessible formats, supported by unmatched customer care.

To order any Aspen Publishers title, go to *www.aspenpublishers.com* or call 1-800-638-8437.

To reinstate your manual update service, call 1-800-638-8437.

For more information on Loislaw products, go to *www.loislaw.com* or call 1-800-364-2512.

For Customer Care issues, e-mail CustomerCare@aspenpublishers.com; call 1-800-234-1660; or fax 1-800-901-9075.

Aspen Publishers
A Wolters Kluwer Company

CONTENTS

INTRODUCTION

Case File II is the second in the series, *Practicing Persuasive Written and Oral Advocacy*. Like *Case File I*, this book is based on *Coburn v. Martinez*, a former psychiatric patient's lawsuit seeking to prevent a journalist from publishing confidential records of the patient's psychotherapy sessions.

While *Case File I* focused on issues of personal jurisdiction and service of process, *Case File II* deals with freedom of speech and of the press under the First Amendment, and also raises a novel issue of vicarious liability for an intentional tort.

In this introduction, we summarize the story of *Coburn v. Martinez*, discuss the structure and theory of *Case File II*, and describe various uses of *Case File II* in the law school curriculum.

Coburn v. Martinez: The Story

Six years ago, Mary Jo Coburn, a diminutive rookie police officer in Dewey City, New York, fatally shot an unarmed prisoner in the back. Her department and the DA's office investigated the shooting and exonerated her. The dead man's family settled its multimillion dollar lawsuit against her with an agreement to seal the records of the case.

Wally Martinez, an investigative journalist, was perplexed by contradictions in the story.

Traumatized by the killing, Coburn sought help from Dr. Christal Plano, a psychiatrist, with whom she shared her troubled feelings and darkest secrets.

After recovering from the emotional trauma of the killing, Coburn resigned from the police department, went back home to Tennessee, completed college, and began a career as a school teacher. Within two years, however, she felt drawn back to her original calling and decided to reenter police work.

Upon learning of Coburn's aspiration to resume work as a police officer, Dr. Plano, her former psychiatrist, vowed to thwart her plans. In a bizarre series of events, Dr. Plano leaked audiotapes of Coburn's most revealing psychotherapy sessions to Martinez, the journalist.

The leaked tapes apparently contain the solution to the mysteries that baffled Martinez: What really led to the killing? Was there a police cover-up? If so, why?

Martinez would score a huge journalistic coup if he could upload the tapes of Coburn's psychiatric confessions to his Web site, which specializes in exposing police misconduct. But before he could do so, Coburn got wind of his plan and sued for an injunction to stop the publication.

Is Martinez liable for the psychiatrist's breach of her fiduciary duty of confidentiality to Coburn? Even if he is, doesn't the First Amendment protect the journalist's publication of this newsworthy information? Those are the cutting-edge legal issues raised in *Case File II*.

Structure and Theory of *Case File II*

Case File II contains a sophisticated and realistic set of litigation documents for practicing written and oral advocacy. The legal documents include a complaint, a motion to dismiss, and an answer, as well as motions for a temporary restraining order and a preliminary injunction.

Evidentiary materials include Coburn's detailed declaration setting forth the background of the case, Martinez's original newspaper articles about the shooting and its aftermath, and an 84-page transcript of trial testimony.

Exercises using these materials may consist of one or two memoranda and oral arguments before the trial court as well as briefs and oral arguments before a court of appeals.

A detailed Teacher's Manual guides the instructor in creating assignments of varying degrees of complexity. Included in the Teacher's Manual are research files for assignments without research components and alternative court opinions for disposing of motions in ways that fit the particular course and support the instructor's teaching objectives. The court opinions are available for distribution to the class according to the instructor's educational objectives and strategy.

Coburn v. Martinez is set in a United States district court because federal rules of practice are familiar and easily accessible to most law students. A full record is developed in the trial court so that students can learn to argue both legal and factual issues, pore over the record to tease out those issues, find evidentiary support for advantageous positions, and grapple realistically with the challenges of standard of review and harmless error.

The case is designed to culminate in a court of appeals, rather than the Supreme Court of the United States, because advocacy before a court of appeals is typical of real-life litigation practice, the issues are more down-to-earth, and the doctrine of precedent is more robust.

Uses of *Case File II*

These materials were created to support an innovative required course in Appellate Advocacy at the University of the Pacific McGeorge School of Law. In that course, which spans two semesters, each student writes two memoranda in the trial court and a full appellate brief, orally argues two motions in the trial court, argues the appeal, and has many opportunities to prepare short written exercises, revise written work, and practice oral arguments. Students' practical exercises are supported by didactic readings[1] on effective advocacy, interactive lectures, and weekly workshops.

Case File II also supports shorter courses in Legal Process, Persuasive Writing, and Pre-Trial Practice, as well as moot court programs. The Teacher's Manual suggests how instructors can use these materials for a variety of courses and teaching objectives.

---

[1] We use Michael R. Fontham, Michael Vitiello & David W. Miller, *Persuasive Written & Oral Advocacy in Trial & Appellate Courts* (Aspen Law & Business, 2002, ISBN 0-7355-2450-5).

This book consists entirely of simulated legal documents. They are simulated because actual documents seldom work well to achieve precise teaching objectives. The documents need to be crafted for educational purposes.

That the documents are simulated does not mean they are unrealistic. On the contrary, the documents in *Case File II* are exactingly similar in both content and form to documents generated in real litigation. The facts of *Coburn v. Martinez* are drawn from actual cases.

Case File II contains no notes, comments, or other aids. Real litigation lacks those amenities. The instructor must decide what forms of assistance students should receive. Several models are included in the Teacher's Manual.

To avoid obsolescence, all dates are adjustable. "YR-00" refers to the year in which you are using the book. "YR-01" means one year earlier. Thus, if you are using the book in 2004, "YR-01" means 2003, "YR-02" means 2002, and so forth. You may find it helpful to make a chart that correlates relative and real years.

Because events in the case file can take place in any real year, no days of the week are indicated. Therefore, there should be no room to argue that described events could not have occurred on the date indicated (*e.g.*, trials are not usually held on Sunday).

We have made every effort to achieve consistency and coherence in *Case File II*. If you notice any anomalies, please let us know. Professor Miller is the managing agent for such matters. He may be reached at (916) 739-7006 or by e-mail at dmiller@uop.edu. We hope you enjoy working with *Case File II*.

D.W.M.

M.V.

M.R.F.

Practicing Persuasive Written and Oral Advocacy

Case File II

Ford & Burns
Phelps Building
233 Dodge Street
Dewey City, New York 13213
Telephone: (891) 776-5400

Elizabeth Ford
Attorney for Plaintiff,
Mary Jo Coburn

```
UNITED STATES DISTRICT COURT
          FILED
     April 10, YR-00
CENTRAL DISTRICT OF NEW YORK
```

In the
UNITED STATES DISTRICT COURT
FOR THE CENTRAL DISTRICT OF NEW YORK

MARY JO COBURN	)	
	)	
Plaintiff	)	
	)	Civil Action No. **00-386 JDS**
vs.	)	
	)	Judge: _John Dell Small, Jr._
WALLY MARTINEZ	)	
	)	
Defendant	)	

COMPLAINT FOR DECLARATORY AND INJUNCTIVE RELIEF AND FOR DAMAGES FOR BREACH OF FIDUCIARY DUTY OF CONFIDENTIALITY

Jurisdiction

1. Plaintiff, Mary Jo Coburn, is a citizen of the State of Tennessee. Defendant,

Wally Martinez, is a citizen of the State of New York. The matter in controversy

exceeds, exclusive of interest and costs, the sum of seventy-five thousand dollars.

[Document page 1]

Common Facts

2.   At various times between approximately July 3, YR-06, and September 29, YR-04, in Dewey City, New York, Plaintiff was a patient in psychotherapeutic treatment with Christal Plano, M.D. (hereinafter "Dr. Plano"), a psychiatrist licensed to practice medicine and psychotherapy under the laws of the State of New York.

3. During the course of psychotherapeutic treatment, Plaintiff disclosed to Dr. Plano numerous private, intimate, and secret matters about herself and her life, including private thoughts, fantasies, wishes, dreams, experiences, and other extremely personal and sensitive matters.

4. Plaintiff made the disclosures referred to in paragraph 3, above, in reliance on Dr. Plano's representation and promise that these disclosures were confidential, were legally protected as privileged communications, and would be disclosed to no other person.

5. Plaintiff's disclosures referred to in paragraph 3, above, were made in the presence of no other person than her psychotherapist, Dr. Plano, were confidential, and are protected by law as privileged and confidential communications.

6. With Plaintiff's consent, Dr. Plano made audiotape recordings of all of Plaintiff's psychotherapy sessions with Dr. Plano. Plaintiff is informed and believes that the

purpose of these tape recordings was to assist Dr. Plano in diagnosing and treating the psychiatric condition for which Plaintiff sought psychotherapeutic treatment.

7. The tape recordings referred to in paragraph 6, above, were and are part of the confidential medical records that Dr. Plano maintains with respect to her diagnosis and treatment of Plaintiff, were not intended to be disclosed or disseminated to any other person, were confidential, and are protected by law as privileged communications.

8. Sometime between March 15, YR-00, and April 3, YR-00, Defendant obtained a copy or copies (hereinafter referred to as "the tapes") of one or more of the tape recordings referred to in paragraph 6, above.

9. When Defendant obtained the tapes, he knew that the contents consisted of confidential communications between Plaintiff and her psychotherapist.

10. Defendant obtained the tapes as the result of a breach by Dr. Plano (or one or more of Dr. Plano's agents or servants acting within the scope of their employment or agency) of the fiduciary duty of confidentiality owed by Dr. Plano to Plaintiff.

11. Defendant has threatened and continues to threaten to publish the contents of the tapes in one or more mass communications media, which media are accessible to and are watched, read, and heard by numerous persons throughout

the states of New York and Tennessee, the United States, and the world. Such publication would violate Plaintiff's legal rights set forth in paragraphs 4, 5, and 10, above.

12.   Defendant has the present ability to carry out his threats to publish the tapes because Defendant owns and operates a site on the World Wide Web, which is marketed to and is accessible to persons with Internet service throughout the states of New York and Tennessee, the United States, and the world.

13.   If Defendant is not restrained and enjoined from publishing the tapes, Plaintiff is informed and believes that Defendant will immediately carry out his threats to publish them.

14.   As a result of Defendant's actions alleged in paragraphs 8 through 13, above, Plaintiff has been subjected to extreme emotional distress and embarrassment.

15.   If Defendant publishes the tapes, as he has threatened, Plaintiff will be further humiliated and embarrassed, will be held up to public ridicule, obloquy, and contempt, will suffer extreme and irreparable mental anguish and distress, will be injured in her ability to secure and retain gainful employment, and will be otherwise gravely and irreparably damaged by the disclosure of her legally privileged confidential communications with her psychiatrist.

16.   Plaintiff has no adequate remedy at law to prevent the damage alleged in paragraph 15, above.

Count One

17.   Paragraphs 1-16, above, are incorporated by reference herein. Defendant is liable to Plaintiff for Dr. Plano's breach of her fiduciary duty of confidentiality to Plaintiff because Defendant, with knowledge of Dr. Plano's fiduciary duty of confidentiality to Plaintiff, solicited and induced Dr. Plano's breach of her fiduciary duty of confidentiality to Plaintiff.

Count Two

18.   Paragraphs 1-16, above, are incorporated by reference herein. In the alternative, Defendant is liable to Plaintiff for Dr. Plano's breach of her fiduciary duty of confidentiality to Plaintiff because Defendant conspired and acted in concert with Dr. Plano in causing, and in carrying out the purposes of, Dr. Plano's breach of her fiduciary duty of confidentiality to Plaintiff.

Count Three

19.   Paragraphs 1-16, above, are incorporated by reference herein. In the alternative, Defendant is liable to Plaintiff for Dr. Plano's breach of her fiduciary duty of confidentiality to Plaintiff because Defendant, being aware of Dr. Plano's breach,

knowingly received a benefit as a result of that breach, namely, valuable information for a news story in his professional capacity as a journalist.

<u>Prayer for Relief</u>

WHEREFORE, Plaintiff prays for a judgment—

A. Declaring that any and all tape recordings of psychotherapeutic sessions between Plaintiff and Christal Plano, M.D., and copies thereof, are privileged confidential communications that cannot lawfully be disclosed by or to anyone without Plaintiff's consent and cannot lawfully be possessed by anyone other than Plaintiff without Plaintiff's consent;

B. Requiring Defendant, temporarily during the pendency of this action and permanently thereafter, to turn over to Plaintiff any and all copies of tape recordings, in Defendant's possession or under Defendant's control, of psychotherapeutic sessions between Plaintiff and Christal Plano, M.D.;

C. Enjoining Defendant and all persons acting in concert with Defendant, temporarily during the pendency of this action and permanently thereafter, from publishing, disseminating, or otherwise disclosing any tape recordings of psychotherapeutic sessions between Plaintiff and Christal Plano, M.D., on any site on the World Wide Web, or in any newspaper, magazine, television or radio program, or in any other medium of communication;

[Document page 6]

D. Awarding Plaintiff compensatory damages in such amount as the court shall

determine to compensate Plaintiff for her damages as alleged herein;

E. Awarding Plaintiff punitive damages to punish Defendant for his unlawful and

outrageous misconduct;

F. Awarding Plaintiff her costs of suit and reasonable attorneys' fees; and

G. Awarding such other and further relief to which Plaintiff may be entitled.

Dated: April 8, YR-00

Respectfully submitted,

Elizabeth Ford

Ford & Burns
Phelps Building
233 Dodge Street
Dewey City, New York 13213

Elizabeth Ford
Attorney for Plaintiff,
Mary Jo Coburn

[Summons and Return of Service omitted.]

Ford & Burns
Phelps Building
233 Dodge Street
Dewey City, New York 13213
Telephone: (891) 776-5400

> UNITED STATES DISTRICT COURT
> **FILED**
> April 10, YR-00
> CENTRAL DISTRICT OF NEW YORK

Elizabeth Ford
Attorney for Plaintiff,
Mary Jo Coburn

In the
UNITED STATES DISTRICT COURT
FOR THE CENTRAL DISTRICT OF NEW YORK

MARY JO COBURN)
)
    Plaintiff)
)
             Civil Action No. **00-386** JDS
vs.)
)
             Judge: _John Dell Small, Jr._
WALLY MARTINEZ)
)
    Defendant)

MOTION FOR A TEMPORARY RESTRAINING ORDER
AND PRELIMINARY INJUNCTION

TO WALLY MARTINEZ, Defendant:

PLEASE TAKE NOTICE that at ___2:00 p.m.___ on April 10, YR-00, or as soon

thereafter as counsel may be heard by the above-entitled court, located at Suite 200,

Old Post Office Building, 607 Victoria Street, Dewey City, New York 13213, in the

[Document page 1]

courtroom of the Honorable ___John Dell Small, Jr.___, United States District

Judge, Plaintiff will and hereby does move the court for a TEMPORARY

RESTRAINING ORDER, pursuant to Fed. R. Civ. P. 65, and thereafter for a

PRELIMINARY INJUNCTION to remain in effect until the final disposition of this

action, restraining and enjoining you, your agents, servants, employees, and

attorneys, and all others acting in concert with you or them, from publishing in any

medium (including but not limited to newspapers, magazines, radio, television, or

any site on the World Wide Web or other place on the communications system

known as the Internet), disseminating, or in any other manner revealing or disclosing

to yourself or to any other person the contents of any audiotape recording (or copy

thereof) of psychotherapeutic sessions between the Plaintiff, Mary Jo Coburn, and

her psychotherapist, Christal Plano, M.D., or any other source of information over

which you have control or to which you have access that embodies or otherwise

evidences confidential communications between the Plaintiff, Mary Jo Coburn, and

the said Christal Plano, M.D., during the course of psychotherapy, and requiring you

to turn over to the custody of the Plaintiff, Mary Jo Coburn, any and all audiotape

recordings or copies of audiotape recordings purporting to be recordings of

psychotherapeutic sessions between the Plaintiff, Mary Jo Coburn, and the said

[Document page 2]

Christal Plano, M.D., pending the hearing and disposition of Plaintiff's Motion for Preliminary Injunction.

This motion is brought on the following grounds: that the Defendant, Wally Martinez, has unlawfully gained possession of copies of tape recordings of privileged and confidential communications between Plaintiff and her psychotherapist, Dr. Plano, and has unlawfully threatened to publish the said tape recordings in various communications media, including the World Wide Web, which are accessible to innumerable persons throughout the states of New York and Tennessee, as well as throughout the world, and if Defendant is not immediately restrained and enjoined from publishing the said tape recordings, Plaintiff will be gravely and irreparably damaged as alleged in paragraph 15 of the Complaint herein and as more fully described in the Declaration of Mary Jo Coburn, filed herewith and incorporated by reference herein.

This motion is based on the Declaration of Mary Jo Coburn and the Memorandum of Points and Authorities filed herewith, the pleadings and other papers on file herein, and such other matters as may be presented to the court at the time of the hearing.

[Document page 3]

Dated: April 8, YR-00

Respectfully submitted,

Elizabeth Ford

Elizabeth Ford

Ford & Burns
Phelps Building
233 Dodge Street
Dewey City, New York 13213
Telephone: (891) 776-5400

Attorney for Plaintiff,
Mary Jo Coburn

CERTIFICATE OF SERVICE

I certify that I am counsel of record for the plaintiff in the above-captioned cause and that I caused the foregoing Motion for a Temporary Restraining Order and Preliminary Injunction, together with the Declaration of Mary Jo Coburn in Support of Plaintiff's Motion for a Temporary Restraining Order, and Exhibit A thereto, to be served upon the defendant by causing copies thereof to be hand-delivered to him at the offices of his attorney, Dean Manning, at 3875 Trupers Pike, in Dewey City, New York this 10th day of April, YR-00, at 9:42 a.m.

Elizabeth Ford

Elizabeth Ford

Ford & Burns
Phelps Building
233 Dodge Street
Dewey City, New York 13213
Telephone: (891) 776-5400

Attorney for Plaintiff,
Mary Jo Coburn

Ford & Burns
Phelps Building
233 Dodge Street
Dewey City, New York 13213
Telephone: (891) 776-5400

Elizabeth Ford
Attorney for Plaintiff,
Mary Jo Coburn

In the
UNITED STATES DISTRICT COURT
FOR THE CENTRAL DISTRICT OF NEW YORK

MARY JO COBURN   )
)
          Plaintiff   )
)
)   Civil Action No. **00-386** JDS
vs.   )
)   Judge: _John Dell Small, Jr._
WALLY MARTINEZ   )
)
          Defendant   )

DECLARATION OF MARY JO COBURN
IN SUPPORT OF PLAINTIFF'S MOTION
FOR A TEMPORARY RESTRAINING ORDER

1. I, Mary Jo Coburn, am the plaintiff in this action against Wally Martinez. Mr.

Martinez is threatening to publish on his World Wide Web site tape recordings of my

psychotherapy sessions with my psychiatrist, Dr. Christine Plano. I am horrified that

anyone would be so cruel as to broadcast to the whole world another person's

[Document page 1]

confidential and privileged statements to her psychiatrist.   I make this declaration to

describe the devastating effect that Mr. Martinez's threatened actions will have on me

if he is not restrained by order of this court.   I also describe the background of this

case and why I believe that a temporary restraining order, preliminary injunction, and

permanent injunctive relief are needed to prevent me from being grievously and

irreparably harmed by Defendant's threatened unlawful conduct.

2. I was born in YR-29 in Nashville, Tennessee, and grew up in Nashville and New

Taft, Tennessee.   I graduated third in my class from New Taft High School in YR-11.

After high school, I moved to Dewey City, New York, where I enrolled in a two-year

Criminal Justice Associates Degree program at the local community college.   I

graduated with honors from that program in YR-09, and was then hired by the

Dewey City Police Department as a police officer trainee.   Later, my department

sponsored my enrollment in the New York State Police Academy.

3. One of the proudest moments of my life was on April 7, YR-07, when I

graduated from the New York State Police Academy as a Certified Peace Officer and

was formally promoted to Police Patrol Officer by the Dewey City Police Department.

For the next six months, I was assigned to patrol duty in the Northeast Division of

the Dewey City Police Department.

4. The saddest and most disturbing moment of my life came six months later, on

January 13, YR-06, when during the course of my duties as a police officer, I had to

[Document page 2]

use my service revolver to stop a fleeing felon who had been arrested for a violent crime and placed in my custody. The suspect, whose name was Ubumu Victoire, bolted from my custody in a hospital emergency room after I had removed his handcuffs so that he could get medical treatment. He ran down a hallway and out an exit door. I followed him and warned him to stop or I would shoot, but he did not stop. I drew my service revolver, warned him again, and this time he lunged at me and grabbed for my service revolver. In all honesty, I do not remember whether the single shot that I then fired was intentional or accidental. But my life was in danger from this man, who was much larger than I am. Regrettably, the bullet lodged in Mr. Victoire's heart, and he died moments later.

5. Naturally, my "shooting of an unarmed suspect" received a great deal of press coverage and was controversial for quite a while. Attached to this declaration as Exhibit A are excerpts from the *Dewey City Herald* newspaper coverage of this event and its aftermath. After thorough investigations, I was exonerated of any wrongdoing by both the Dewey County District Attorney's office and the Internal Affairs Division of the Dewey City Police Department. The District Attorney's office declined to prefer any criminal charges against me, and the Police Department cleared me of any violation of departmental rules. (I had been routinely placed on administrative assignment following the shooting of Mr. Victoire.) On February 25, YR-06, I was

returned to unrestricted duty and resumed my assignment as a patrol officer in the Northeast Division.

6. Soon after returning to duty, I began to have nightmares and panic attacks. I started feeling timid and unsure of myself—an extremely disabling attitude for a police officer. On the advice of the police chaplain, I sought out a psychiatrist for treatment. My psychiatrist, Dr. Christal Plano, a medical doctor and licensed physician who practices in Dewey City, recommended psychotherapy ("talk therapy"), which I began in early July, YR-06. Dr. Plano advised me that our conversations would be confidential and would not be disclosed by her to any other living soul except by court order if anything came up that the law would require her to report. The only thing I recall her mentioning along those lines was child abuse. Also, Dr. Plano asked my permission to make an audiotape recording of each of our sessions together. She said the purpose of recording the sessions was to free her from having to take detailed notes, so that she could listen more carefully to what I said and how I said it. She said she would review the tapes from time to time, and that they would be part of my confidential medical records. At first I was nervous about having our conversations taped, but after a while I stopped noticing the tape recorder and came to trust Dr. Plano and her assurances of secrecy.

7. Psychotherapy was an intense experience for me. The things I said in my sessions with Dr. Plano are nobody's business. However, it is well known that

[Document page 4]

patients in psychotherapy often talk about their childhood traumas, their fears, their dreams, their ambitions, their disappointments, their troubled relationships, and difficulties at work. I went to Dr. Plano to work out profound feelings of sadness, shame, and remorse about the shooting of Mr. Victoire. When I shot Mr. Victoire, I believed I had no choice and had done the right thing as a police officer. Nevertheless, it was difficult for me to continue functioning with such self-doubt.

8. With the benefit of Dr. Plano's treatment, my symptoms were gradually improving when, on September 22, YR-06, I was sued by Mr. Victoire's family for $264 million. I was devastated. All the progress I had been making toward regaining my confidence and peace of mind was shattered. Within a month, I had no choice but to request a medical leave of absence from the Dewey City Police Department, which was granted.

9. By March of YR-05, I felt that I had largely recovered from the unpleasant symptoms that drove me to psychotherapy, and I terminated psychotherapy with Dr. Plano. However, by then, I had lost my enthusiasm for police work, and so on April 1, YR-05, I resigned from the Dewey City Police Department.

10. In August YR-05, I moved back home to New Taft, Tennessee, and enrolled as an undergraduate at New Taft State College. I graduated with a Bachelor of Science degree in physical education in December YR-03. From then until June YR-

01, I worked as an assistant coach (soccer, volleyball, and basketball) and physical education teacher in the New Taft Union School District.

11.   Meanwhile, the civil action brought against me by Mr. Victoire's family went to trial in Dewey City, New York, in September YR-04. I returned to Dewey City for the trial. As the trial approached, I experienced flashbacks of some of the old problems that had taken me into psychotherapy, so while I was in Dewey City, I saw Dr. Plano for three psychotherapy sessions. On October 3, YR-04, the case of *Victoire v. Coburn* was settled. The settlement included mutual promises of confidentiality, so I am not at liberty to say anything about the settlement. Between YR-04 and YR-00, I gradually forgot about the unpleasant events of YR-06—YR-04.

12.   After teaching for two years, I began to feel a calling back to police work. Police work was the only kind of work I ever wanted to do when I was growing up. I am well trained, and I feel that I have a gift for this kind of work despite the unfortunate events surrounding Mr. Victoire's death. I discussed my interest with the personnel office of the New Taft Police Department, and I was advised that I had a good chance of being hired as a police officer by that department. In view of the incident in New York and my history of psychiatric treatment, I was advised to get a letter from Dr. Plano attesting to my successful completion of psychotherapy and my current mental and emotional fitness to work as a police officer.

[Document page 6]

13.   On March 8, YR-00, I submitted a formal application to the New Taft Police Department for appointment as a police-patrol officer. On March 15, YR-00, I telephoned Dr. Plano in Dewey City, New York, and requested that she write a letter to the Department on my behalf. She expressed concern about whether I wanted to waive confidentiality as to my medical records of psychotherapy sessions with her. I replied that I did not want to waive confidentiality. She said that she would need some time to consider whether she could write an appropriate letter attesting to my fitness for police work without jeopardizing the confidentiality of my medical records. She also said that she wanted to retrieve my file from storage in order to refresh her memory about the details of my case.

14.   I did not hear from Dr. Plano again until she telephoned me on March 28, YR-00. She told me that she had reason to believe that parts of my confidential medical records had been obtained by an outsider. Specifically, she said that she believed that someone had managed to make a copy of one or more of the tape recordings of my psychotherapy sessions with her. When I asked her why she believed this, she said she had received an anonymous telephone call from a man who played an excerpt of a recording and asked if she could verify that the voices on the recording were those of herself and former police officer Mary Jo Coburn (that's me). Dr. Plano told me that she clearly recognized the voices as mine and hers, talking in a manner and tone that sounded like a psychotherapy session. Dr. Plano

said that the content of the particular segment of the recording that the caller played was innocuous. But the caller told her that it was only a short excerpt from a longer tape (or several tapes) which he had obtained and which he was planning to post on a site on the World Wide Web unless he determined that the recording was counterfeit.

15. I asked Dr. Plano in our telephone conversation on March 28, YR-00, how anyone could have gotten hold of the tapes of my psychotherapy, and she replied that she suspected carelessness (or worse) on the part of Gibraltar Records Management, Inc., in Dewey City, the company with which Dr. Plano told me she contracts for storage of her inactive medical files and records. I gathered that the breach of security occurred sometime after Dr. Plano requested Gibraltar to retrieve my records and deliver them to her.

16. I asked Dr. Plano what she intended to do about this breach of security, and she mentioned something about consulting her lawyer and suggested that I ought to seek legal counsel of my own. Finally, she said that she expected the anonymous caller to call again in the next few days and was hoping that her lawyers would advise her how to handle the matter.

17. On March 30, YR-00, I telephoned Dr. Plano and told her that I wanted to speak directly to the anonymous caller. She said she would try to arrange it. The next day, Dr. Plano called and said the anonymous caller had contacted her again.

[Document page 8]

She said that he was not willing to give out any information by which I could contact him, but Dr. Plano gave him my telephone number in New Taft, and he told her that he would get in touch with me.

18.   Between April 3 and April 5, YR-00, I received at home several telephone calls from a man purporting to be Dr. Plano's anonymous caller. During our conversations, it came out that his name was Wally Martinez. I recognized Mr. Martinez as the reporter for the *Dewey City Herald* who had covered the Victoire shooting and the subsequent civil trial. (His name is on the byline of the newspaper articles attached hereto as Exhibit A.) Mr. Martinez told me that my case had awakened him to (what he regards as) a serious problem in this country with inadequate police officer selection and training standards, excessive police violence, and misuse of firearms by the police. Exposing and crusading against these abuses (as he called them) has become his "mission in life." He said that about three years ago he established a site on the World Wide Web devoted to those issues, known as "www.outlawcops.com."   He told me that in the last year his Web site had received, on average, more than 200 "hits" per day, and that it has become his full-time occupation.

19. In my telephone conversations with Mr. Martinez between April 3 and 5, Mr. Martinez stated that he had acquired the tapes of my psychotherapy sessions with Dr. Plano "legitimately," but refused to give me any details. He said he was planning

[Document page 9]

to publish portions of those tapes on his Web site as part of a documentary and audio-video collection regarding the death of Mr. Victoire. He said that the tapes would "cast a whole new light" on the death of Mr. Victoire. He said that all he needed to ascertain was whether the tapes were authentic.

20.   Throughout our conversations, I pleaded with Mr. Martinez to respect my privacy and the confidentiality of my communications with my psychiatrist, but he was unmoved. I offered to buy the tapes from him, but he refused. I offered to help him locate documentary evidence about the investigation into the death of Mr. Victoire that would be far more interesting and important to him as a journalist, but he was not interested. While Mr. Martinez did have the decency to refrain from doing anything with the tapes while I tried to reason with him over the course of several days, I am convinced that his self-restraint is at an end and that he will imminently make public the contents of my confidential communications with my psychotherapist.

21.   I would be extremely embarrassed to have my psychotherapy sessions broadcast to the entire world on the World Wide Web. Without revealing anything that I told Dr. Plano, I think it is quite understandable that a patient in psychotherapy may have said things to her psychiatrist about people that she would not want to say to their faces. I think it is quite understandable that a patient may say things that would cause people to judge her harshly. I think it is quite understandable that a

[Document page 10]

patient may say things that would jeopardize her present employment and ruin her

future employment prospects. I realize that I may sound cagey, but I am caught

between a rock and a hard place because I do not want to reveal anything that was

said in my psychotherapy sessions with Dr. Plano for fear of being held to have

waived the confidentiality of those sessions. If the court is not satisfied that

publication of the tapes would be extremely embarrassing and stressful to me, I

would be willing to have the court listen to the tapes in chambers if that could be

done with adequate protections against further disclosure. However, I hope that will

not be necessary.

22.   The past two weeks have been hell for me. Mr. Martinez's threat to publish

my psychotherapy sessions for the whole world to eavesdrop on is very distressing. I

have not been able to sleep. I have become obsessed with this problem to the

exclusion of all other activities in my life. I am beset by feelings of fear, shame,

remorse, timidity, and lack of self-confidence. My main source of strength is my

belief that the law surely will not allow Mr. Martinez to <u>rape</u> me (figuratively speaking,

of course, but that is exactly how it feels to me) in front of my friends and family and

a leering worldwide audience in cyberspace.

23.   If Mr. Martinez is allowed to publish the tapes of my psychotherapy sessions,

I cannot imagine any legal remedy that could possibly make me whole. Money

damages could in no way make up for my shame, embarrassment, and utter humiliation. I pleaded with Mr. Martinez to act with ordinary human decency, but he paid no attention to my plea. I pray that this court will listen and understand and stop this tragedy from being inflicted on me. Thank you.

I declare under penalty of perjury that the foregoing is true and correct.

Executed on this 8th day of April, YR-00:

Mary Jo Coburn
Mary Jo Coburn

Respectfully submitted,

Elizabeth Ford
Elizabeth Ford

Ford & Burns
Phelps Building
233 Dodge Street
Dewey City, New York 13213
Telephone: (891) 776-5400

Attorney for Plaintiff,
Mary Jo Coburn

EXHIBIT A TO DECLARATION OF MARY JO COBURN

The Dewey City Herald
January 15, YR-06

Burglary suspect slain by officer was shot in the back as he ran

By Wally Martinez
Herald Staff Writer

A burglary suspect shot and killed by a Dewey City police officer two nights ago as he attempted to escape from custody was struck in the middle of his right back by the bullet, the state medical examiner's office said yesterday.

Ubumu Victoire, 32, of the 8800 block of County Line Road, was shot when he ran from the emergency room of Miseracordia Hospital, where he was being treated for injuries suffered in a fight with at least three police officers who had arrested him, police said.

Police said Officer Mary Jo Coburn, 22, chased Mr. Victoire down a hallway and out of the hospital before she fired a single shot. She had been assigned to guard Mr. Victoire at the hospital after his arrest for a suspected burglary.

Deputy Chief Medical Examiner Donald Wright said the bullet entered Mr. Victoire's back and struck his heart. He was pronounced dead several minutes later inside the hospital.

The manner of the death has been ruled a homicide, the standard medical examiner's ruling whenever one person kills another, Dr. Wright said. But the determination as to whether the homicide is justified is not made by the medical examiner, he said.

Agent Doug Price, a police spokesman, said investigators are conducting an "intensive review" of the shooting and will submit their findings to the state's attorney's office for a ruling on whether Officer Coburn was justified in using deadly force.

Officer Coburn could also face a departmental trial board if it is found that she violated police procedures.

Agent Price refused to talk about witnesses' accounts of the incident or the account of the shooting that Officer Coburn gave to investigators.

Officer Coburn, a two-year veteran of the force assigned to the Northeast District, has been placed on administrative duty pending the outcome of the investigation.

The action is normal department procedure any time an officer is involved in a shooting.

Mr. Victoire was arrested the afternoon of January 13 in a house in the 300 block of N. Calhoun St. after police went there for a report of a burglary. Police said Mr. Victoire, who was hiding in a second-floor bedroom closet, fought with the arresting officers.

He suffered a cut to the head and complained of pain in his shoulder, and police brought him to the hospital to be examined. He bolted from the emergency room when his handcuffs were removed during the examination, police said.

Correctional officials said Mr. Victoire had previously served 17 months at the Intercounty Correctional Institution in Nelson for violating probation on attempted theft and assault convictions.

oOo

[Document page 1]

The Dewey City Herald
January 17, YR-06

Officer says burglary suspect had tried to reach for her gun

By Wally Martinez
Herald Staff Writer

A Dewey City police officer who fatally shot a burglary suspect in the back as he tried to escape from custody told investigators the man stopped suddenly and reached back as though he intended to grab her gun, according to a police report of the incident.

Officer Mary Jo Coburn, 22, claimed to investigating officers that her 9 mm Glock pistol discharged when the victim's hand came in contact with the weapon, the incident report said.

Ubumu Victoire, 32, of the 8800 block of County Line Road, died several minutes later of a bullet wound that entered the middle of the right side of his back and struck his heart, a state medical examiner said.

The fatal shooting occurred January 13 at Miseracordia Hospital, located at 555 Park Terrace Drive, where Mr. Victoire was being treated for minor injuries he suffered in an alleged fight with at least three police officers who had arrested him for a suspected burglary.

According to the incident report, Officer Coburn, a two-year veteran on the Dewey City police department, was assigned to guard Mr. Victoire in the triage room, where she had handcuffed him to a chair while he awaited treatment.

Police said she was the only officer assigned to guard him.

A hospital employee asked Officer Coburn to remove the handcuffs so Mr. Victoire could undergo a blood pressure exam, the report said.

When she removed the handcuffs, Mr. Victoire "bolted from the triage room and ran into the emergency room corridor. Officer Coburn, directly behind him, shouted 'Stop or I'll shoot,'" the report said.

The suspect continued to run, heading down the corridor and eventually out the door to the ambulance area in front of the emergency room, the report said.

The officer, following close behind him, the report said, again shouted "Stop or I'll shoot."

"At this point [Mr. Victoire] stopped and rapidly began to turn towards his right and towards Officer Coburn," the report said of her account. Mr. Victoire "had his right hand out and extended and was swinging his arm around" toward her, she told investigators.

The officer had her right hand—which held the pistol—extended toward Mr. Victoire; she was "fearing for her life," the report said.

oOo

The Dewey City Herald
February 7, YR-06

Officer not charged in fatal shooting; in-house inquiry planned in death

By Wally Martinez
Herald Staff Writer

A young Dewey City police officer cleared of criminal charges now faces a departmental inquiry into the fatal shooting of a burglary suspect who broke free from her custody at Miseracordia Hospital January 13.

[Document page 2]

Although the state's attorney said criminal charges will not be filed against Officer Mary Jo Coburn, 22, department investigators are focusing on several questions, including why Officer Coburn had her gun drawn.

Ubumu Victoire, 32, of the 8800 block of County Line Road, was shot by Officer Coburn after he fled from the Miseracordia emergency room.

Mr. Victoire was being treated there for minor injuries from a scuffle with three other officers who had arrested him in a burglary.

Officer Coburn told investigators that Mr. Victoire stopped suddenly and reached back as if he were trying to grab for her gun. Her 9 mm Glock pistol fired when it came into contact with Mr. Victoire's hand, a police report said.

Dewey City State's Attorney Stuart O. Simms said the autopsy report, which showed gunpowder residue on Mr. Victoire's hands, and an eyewitness statement supported Officer Coburn's account.

"It was our conclusion that there was insufficient evidence to warrant further investigation at this time," Mr. Simms said yesterday. "Based on that we have referred the matter to the Police Department for whatever action they deem appropriate."

Police Department officials would not comment for the record, except to say that the investigation into the shooting is continuing. But departmental sources said several mistakes apparently were made before the shooting. They included:

- Arresting officers did not tell Officer Coburn why Mr. Victoire had been arrested.

- Officer Coburn should not have been left alone with Mr. Victoire, especially after he had scuffled with officers.

- Officers also should have put leg irons on Mr. Victoire in the emergency room, where handcuffs are commonly removed to facilitate medical treatment.

oOo

The Dewey City Herald
September 23, YR-06

Suit filed in killing by police officer

By Wally Martinez
Herald Staff Writer

Attorneys for the family of a man shot in the back and killed while he attempted to flee from a Dewey City police officer in January have filed a $264 million lawsuit, charging that "excessive deadly force" was used.

The lawsuit, filed yesterday in Dewey County Court, alleges that Officer Mary Jo Coburn took aim at the fleeing man, Ubumu Victoire, and fired even though she knew he was unarmed.

Mr. Victoire, 32, of the 8800 block of County Line Road, was arrested on a burglary charge January 13 and suffered injuries in a fight with police. He was taken to Miseracordia Hospital to be treated, and Officer Coburn, 22, was assigned as the lone person to guard him.

After hospital personnel removed his handcuffs to take his blood pressure, Mr. Victoire bolted from the emergency room and ran down a hallway with Officer Coburn in pursuit, according to a police report.

The officer claimed her 9 mm Glock pistol discharged when Mr. Victoire stopped suddenly and attempted to grab the weapon, the police report said. A police review of the incident concluded that the shooting was justified, and

[Document page 3]

the state's attorney's office did not file criminal charges.

But the lawsuit takes issue with the claim that Mr. Victoire tried to grab the weapon. Dwayne Brown, an attorney for Mr. Victoire's family, called Officer Coburn's claim "a fabrication." Mr. Brown pointed to an autopsy report by the state medical examiner's office, which concluded that Mr. Victoire's bullet wound "demonstrated neither evidence of close range nor contact firing."

The lawsuit said Mr. Victoire was running away in fear and posed no threat to the officer. The officer, the lawsuit said, "owed a duty to Mr. Victoire to exercise her authority in a reasonable manner. . . . [She] had a duty to use only such force as was reasonable."

Named as defendants are Officer Coburn, the city Police Department and Commissioner Patrick Connally, and the State of New York.

oOo

The Dewey City Herald
September 27, YR-04

Officer defends fatal shooting

Unarmed suspect was shot in back during chase in YR-06

By Wally Martinez
Herald Staff Writer

In an incident that raised alarms among some commanders in the Dewey City Police Department, a rookie officer who shot an unarmed suspect in the back and killed him in YR-06 went on trial yesterday to defend herself against a lawsuit charging her with wrongful death.

In opening arguments in Dewey County Court, attorneys for the family of Ubumu Victoire claimed that their client's death was the result of a "cold-blooded" shooting by Officer Mary Jo Coburn and asked that the jury award damages.

"There's no dispute that he wasn't armed," attorney Rawles C. Blaisdell told the jury. "He didn't have a knife, a stick, anything. And she shot him in the back. I want you to think about that."

Officer Coburn's attorney told the jury he would prove that his client fired in self-defense after Mr. Victoire spun around while the officer was chasing him and tried to grab her gun.

Officer Coburn was a 22-year-old, slightly built rookie six months out of the police academy when she climbed into a police wagon the evening of January 13, YR-06, to escort a prisoner to Miseracordia Hospital for treatment.

Mr. Victoire, 32, a construction worker and father of three with a minor criminal record, sat quietly in the back of the van. A burglary suspect, he was taken into custody less than an hour earlier and beaten by police, who said he resisted arrest.

Officer Coburn was not involved in the arrest and had no idea what the charges were against Mr. Victoire. She would later describe her prisoner as cooperative, almost cordial. But a few minutes later, he broke free of her in the hospital and, after a brief chase, she shot him on the street outside.

The Police Department ruled that it was reasonable under the circumstances for her to shoot her 9 mm pistol almost point-blank into Victoire's back because there was evidence that he was spinning around and reaching for the gun when she pulled the trigger.

The Department and then-Commissioner Patrick Connally were named as co-defendants in the suit, but were later dismissed from the case on grounds that they have immunity as state officials, court records show.

But the shooting was emblematic of larger problems in the department at the time, records show. Not the least of the questions raised by the case was why a rookie officer had been left alone to guard a prisoner who supposedly had resisted arrest by at least three veteran police officers an hour earlier.

The killing of Ubumu Victoire also took place during one of the deadliest periods in history on the streets of Dewey City. It was a time when city police were shooting unarmed suspects at a record rate—at least nine were killed or injured from YR-08 to YR-06—in a sharp increase in the use of deadly force.

For years, the department had been logging slightly more than six shootings by its officers annually. And they almost always involved armed opponents. Then, in YR-08, the number of suspects killed and injured began to rise. By YR-07, 16 people had been shot. Another 15 were hit the year Officer Coburn shot Ubumu Victoire.

The official response by police commanders was that the streets were becoming more dangerous and suspects were becoming better armed.

But in memos and reports from the department's internal investigation division, some administrators were warning that the increase was at least partly attributable to the fact that the department was absorbing one of the biggest surges in rookie officers in its history, and veterans were retiring in record numbers. The trend continues today.

By YR-02, nearly three out of four Dewey City police officers will have less than five years' experience, the department estimates. Among other indications of the impact of novice police officers is the record rate at which they have been wrecking police cars.

Records show that they also account for about half the uses of deadly force.

Faced with such evidence, Police Commissioner Constantine Callas began to clamp down on the use of force by his officers as soon as he arrived in YR-05. And the number of shootings fell almost overnight—with no increase in injuries to officers.

Tougher rules on when officers can pull the trigger, a liberal policy on the use of nonlethal pepper Mace, and a new requirement of mandatory disciplinary action for clumsy police officers who shoot accidentally cut in half the number of deaths and injuries to civilians by this year.

To date, about seven suspects have been shot in YR-04—a number roughly equivalent to the department's level in YR-10, before rookies began to flood the streets.

But on January 13, YR-06, neither Officer Coburn nor Mr. Victoire had the benefit of the new rules and tougher standards.

After arriving at the Scotland Street entrance to Miseracordia Hospital about 4:30 p.m., Officer Coburn handcuffed Mr. Victoire by his right wrist to a chair in the emergency room to await an evaluation. Soon, a nurse arrived and asked the officer to take off the cuff so Mr. Victoire's blood pressure could be taken.

The test completed, Officer Coburn turned to put the handcuffs back on her prisoner. Mr. Victoire shoved her, then bolted down a corridor for the door.

"He was running like he meant to go somewhere," the nurse, Victor Simpkins, testified yesterday. "He looked to me like he was trying to get away, to escape."

"Stop or I'll shoot you!" several witnesses recalled the officer yelling as she charged after Mr. Victoire with her gun still in its holster. "Stop now!"

[Document page 5]

As she ran out the door five feet behind Mr. Victoire, she pulled out her pistol, a bystander testified.

"It was in her hand, but it was at her side," said Bowman R. O'Neill, a 28-year-old electrician who had taken his daughter to the hospital for some tests. "After that, all I saw was her back when she went by me. Then I heard the shot."

Mr. Simpkins, the nurse, ran after the officer to find her standing over Mr. Victoire's body on the pavement. The bullet had torn through his spine and one lung and had come to a stop in his heart. He died in less than a minute.

"Isn't it true that you shot him because you knew you'd be in big trouble if he got away from you?" demanded Mr. Blaisdell, attorney for the Victoire family.

"No, that's not correct," Officer Coburn replied tersely.

Testimony in the case is expected to continue for the rest of the week.

oOo

The Dewey City Herald
September 28, YR-04

Procedural Lapses Led to Man's Death, Experts Say

Witnesses testify in suit filed by family of suspect who was slain by officer

By Wally Martinez
Herald Staff Writer

Ubumu Victoire should not be dead.

So say two witnesses who testified yesterday in Dewey County Court, where the family of Mr. Victoire is suing a city police officer for shooting the 32-year-old construction worker and father of three in the back and killing him.

The witnesses were a former Boston police chief testifying as a paid expert for the plaintiffs and a security guard who saw Officer Mary Jo Coburn pull the trigger.

The former chief said lax policies and lapses in judgment by Dewey City police commanders created a situation that was ripe for disaster long before the fatal shot was fired. And the security guard said he was alarmed when Mr. Victoire—a prisoner who had been brought to a hospital for treatment—was left unshackled in the emergency room by Officer Coburn.

As a result, the 22-year-old rookie, six months out of the police academy, was left with a terrible choice when Mr. Victoire bolted from custody on January 13, YR-06.

"It's unfortunate, because it was circumstances not of her making," said former police chief Arnold Bright in an interview outside the courtroom.

The department and then-commissioner Patrick Connally were originally named as co-defendants, but were dismissed when a judge ruled they are immune as state officials. And none of the police supervisors involved were disciplined because the department ruled that the shooting was justified, said police spokesman Perry Spencer.

Back in the courtroom, the day's testimony ended with Officer Coburn taking the stand.

The mother of two said she reported to the Northeast District station about 4 p.m. that day, expecting to spend the night riding with a veteran officer and learning the ropes—only to be told to escort an injured prisoner to Miseracordia Hospital.

[Document page 6]

Mr. Victoire had been arrested an hour earlier as a burglary suspect and beaten by police who said he resisted arrest.

But no one told Officer Coburn about the incident or what the charges were against Mr. Victoire, she testified.

At the hospital, she said, a nurse asked her to remove Mr. Victoire's handcuffs for a blood pressure test. He had been cooperative, Officer Coburn testified, so she did so.

Down the hallway, security guard Placencio Aruga, 32, viewed the situation differently: "I was surprised he wasn't in leg irons," he testified, because officers usually shackled prisoners before taking off the handcuffs.

"That got my attention right away," he said later in an interview. "He wouldn't have been able to go anywhere if he had the leg irons on."

The Dewey City Police Manual leaves it up to officers whether to use leg irons. Police said the policy remains unchanged—despite several escape attempts in area hospitals in recent years.

Unfettered, Mr. Victoire rose from his chair after his examination and shoved Officer Coburn—then ran down an 85-foot hallway, through two automatic doors and out onto Scotland Street with the rookie in hot pursuit.

Suddenly, Mr. Victoire stopped, spun to his right and raised his arm, the officer testified.

"I can't recall when I drew my weapon," said Officer Coburn. "I had my weapon up and his hand came right towards it. I ducked and the gun discharged. I don't have a recollection of actually pulling the trigger."

But, she added, she "honestly believed he was going to take my weapon and use it on me. I had a split second to decide."

Former police chief Bright testified that an officer may use deadly force only to prevent someone from causing death or serious injury to another, or to stop a violent felon from escaping.

Anything else is negligence or worse.

"In this case, she had no idea what the suspect had been charged with," he testified, and Mr. Victoire had not threatened anyone up to the moment the gun went off. "It is not clear whether she fired the weapon accidentally," he said.

Afterward, in an interview, Mr. Bright said that compound lapses in Dewey City Police Department procedures were partly to blame.

In not requiring leg irons and leaving a rookie alone to handle a prisoner charged with violently resisting arrest, police supervisors flirted with disaster.

"That should not happen in a well-organized police department," he said.

oOo

The Dewey City Herald
September 30, YR-04

Expert disputes police evidence in shooting of prisoner by officer

By Wally Martinez
Herald Staff Writer

The evidence used by the Dewey City Police Department to exonerate Officer Mary Jo Coburn when she shot an unarmed man in the back in YR-06 came under attack in a Dewey

County Court civil trial this week by experts testifying for the dead man's family.

Yesterday, in the fourth and final day of testimony in a lawsuit brought by the wife and children of Ubumu Victoire, the deceased man, a key forensics witness for the plaintiffs blasted the department's central finding in the case.

Within a few days after the January 13, YR-06, slaying, police ruled that Ms. Coburn had fired in self-defense when Mr. Victoire—an escaped prisoner who bolted away from the officer when she took him to Miseracordia Hospital for medical treatment—turned and tried to grab her 9 mm Glock pistol.

To support the claim, police said they had recovered traces of gunshot residue from Mr. Victoire's hand that could only have gotten there if his hand was near the gun when it went off. The finding, they said, confirmed Officer Coburn's account of the shooting.

But Dr. John Steiner, a former chief forensic scientist for the New Hampshire State Police, testified as a paid expert for Mr.Victoire's family that the traces were so minuscule that they could not support the officer's account of a point-blank self-defense gunshot.

Jury deliberations will begin tomorrow.

oOo

The Dewey City Herald
October 4, YR-04

Police Shooting Case Settled

By Wally Martinez
Herald Staff Writer

The lawsuit over a police killing of an unarmed suspect has been settled.

Lawyers for the family of the late Ubumu Victoire and Officer Mary Jo Coburn announced the settlement to a stunned courtroom yesterday afternoon. The case had been scheduled to go to the jury that morning.

Terms of the settlement were not revealed. A courthouse source disclosed that the settlement was worked out in secret negotiations over the weekend. The final settlement provided that none of the parties or lawyers would reveal the terms and nature of the settlement.

In an unusual move, County Court Judge Harold Reiser ordered that the settlement and all other records in the case be permanently sealed.

oOo

In the
UNITED STATES DISTRICT COURT
FOR THE CENTRAL DISTRICT OF NEW YORK

MARY JO COBURN   )

Plaintiff   )

vs.   )

WALLY MARTINEZ   )

Defendant   )

> **UNITED STATES DISTRICT COURT**
> **FILED**
> **April 10, YR-00**
> **CENTRAL DISTRICT OF NEW YORK**

Civil Action No. 00-386 JDS

Judge: John Dell Small, Jr.

TEMPORARY RESTRAINING ORDER AND ORDER TO SHOW CAUSE

This cause came on to be heard this 10th day of April, YR-00, on Plaintiff's Motion for a Temporary Restraining Order. Defendant was given actual notice of Plaintiff's motion by personal service of the notice of this motion along with the summons and complaint in this action. Defendant appeared through counsel and participated at the hearing on Plaintiff's motion.

The court has considered Plaintiff's Motion for a Temporary Restraining Order, the declaration filed in support of said motion, and the arguments of counsel, and being fully advised, makes the following findings of fact, conclusions of law, and orders.

[Document page 1]

Findings of Fact

1. The defendant, Wally Martinez, has acquired copies of audiotape recordings (hereinafter "the recordings") of psychotherapy sessions in Dewey City, New York, between the plaintiff, Mary Jo Coburn, and her psychiatrist, Christal Plano, M.D., which recordings were intended to be confidential and were made under such circumstances as to create in the plaintiff a justifiable and reasonable expectation of confidentiality and privacy;

2. When the defendant acquired the said recordings, he knew or should have known that the recordings contained confidential communications between a psychiatrist and her patient, and he knew or should have known that such communications are legally privileged against disclosure by the laws of the State of New York;

3. The defendant has threatened and continues to threaten to publish the recordings, or substantial excerpts therefrom, in media of mass communications, including the defendant's World Wide Web site on the Internet;

4. If the recordings are published, the plaintiff will be seriously and irreparably harmed, embarrassed, and humiliated by the dissemination of her most intimate secrets, which she divulged to her psychiatrist in reliance upon assurances of confidentiality and upon the New York law of privilege for confidential communications between psychiatrists and their patients;

5. If the defendant is restrained from publishing the recordings, the defendant may be slightly injured in that he may be impeded or delayed in the practice of his profession as a journalist, but the injury to the defendant will not be serious or irreparable because the news

[Document page 2]

value of the recordings will not significantly diminish during the period in which a temporary restraining order will remain in effect;

6. If the defendant is restrained from publishing the recordings, the public interest may be harmed to the extent that the public will be temporarily deprived of information that may be of importance in the evaluation of the qualifications of the plaintiff as a candidate for employment as a police officer in New Taft, Tennessee, and information that may be important in evaluating the efficiency and integrity of police administration in Dewey City, New York. However, any resulting harm to the public interest will not be substantial or irreparable because the events to which the recordings allegedly relate are nearly five years old, and the value of the information allegedly contained on the said recordings will not diminish significantly during the period in which a temporary restraining order will remain in effect;

7. If the defendant is not restrained from publishing the recordings, the public interest will be injured to an indeterminate but potentially significant extent in that the confidentiality of communications between psychiatrists and their patients will be called into question and the efficacy of psychotherapy, which is a socially beneficial process, may be jeopardized.

Conclusions of Law

1. The plaintiff has demonstrated a probability of success on the merits of this action, in that:

a) The unauthorized publication of confidential communications between psychiatrist and patient is actionable under the law of New York, and is subject to being restrained by

[Document page 3]

injunction at least where the publisher is either the psychiatrist or someone acting in concert with the psychiatrist with knowledge of the confidential relationship. *See Doe v. Roe*, 400 N.Y.S.2d 668 (Sup. Ct. 1977).

b) The public interest in the publication of the recordings does not outweigh the harm to the plaintiff and the public interest that would result from publication of the recordings.

2. The plaintiff has demonstrated the requisites for the entry of a temporary restraining order, in that:

a) A temporary restraining order pending the hearing on the plaintiff's motion for preliminary injunction is necessary to maintain the status quo and to prevent grave and irreparable harm to the plaintiff;

b) The plaintiff has no adequate remedy at law;

c) The balance of equities and the public interest favor the granting of a temporary restraining order in this case.

Therefore, it is by the court ordered, adjudged, and decreed:

Temporary Restraining Order

1. The defendant, Wally Martinez, his agents, servants, employees, and attorneys and all persons acting in concert with them are temporarily restrained and enjoined from:

a) publishing in any medium (including but not limited to books, newspapers, magazines, radio, television, or any site on the World Wide Web or other place on the Internet), disseminating, or in any other manner revealing or disclosing to himself or to any other person the contents of any audiotape recording (or copy thereof) of

[Document page 4]

psychotherapeutic sessions between the plaintiff, Mary Jo Coburn, and her psychotherapist, Christal Plano, M.D., or any other source of information over which the defendant has control or to which he has access, that embodies or otherwise evidences confidential communication between the plaintiff, Mary Jo Coburn, and Christal Plano, M.D., during the course of psychotherapy; and

    b) altering, tampering with, destroying, despoiling, erasing, giving away, selling, or in any manner disposing of any audiotape recordings or copies of audiotape recordings purporting to be recordings of psychotherapeutic sessions between the plaintiff, Mary Jo Coburn, and Christal Plano, M.D.; and

2. The defendant is ordered to retain safely and securely in his possession (or in a bank safe deposit box accessible exclusively to the defendant) all such audiotape recordings or copies of audiotape recordings, pending further order of this court.

This Temporary Restraining Order shall be effective on Plaintiff's giving security approved by the court in the sum of Ten Thousand Dollars ($10,000.00) for the payment of such costs and damage as may be incurred or suffered by any party who is found to have been wrongfully enjoined or restrained.

Order to Show Cause

The defendant, Wally Martinez, is hereby ordered to show cause before this court at 9:30 a.m. on April 20, YR-00, or as soon thereafter as counsel may be heard, why a preliminary injunction of like effect as the within Temporary Restraining Order should not be granted and kept in effect until the final determination of this action.

[Document page 5]

The Temporary Restraining Order entered herein shall expire ten days after being entered unless within such time and upon a showing of good cause the order is extended for a like period, or unless the defendant consents that it may be extended for a longer period.

Dated: April 10, YR-00, at 5:17 p.m.

John Dell Small, Jr.
John Dell Small, Jr.
United States District Judge

Injunction bond in the sum of $10,000.00 guaranteed by Federal Fidelity Insurance Co., surety, approved this 11th day of April, YR-00.

John Dell Small, Jr.
John Dell Small, Jr.
United States District Judge

Ford & Burns
Phelps Building
233 Dodge Street
Dewey City, New York 13213
Telephone: (891) 776-5400

Elizabeth Ford
Attorney for Plaintiff,
Mary Jo Coburn

Manning & Kobalewski
3875 Trupers Pike, Suite 211
Dewey City, New York 13213
Telephone (891) 777-6563

Dean Manning
Attorney for Defendant,
Wally Martinez

In the
UNITED STATES DISTRICT COURT
FOR THE CENTRAL DISTRICT OF NEW YORK

MARY JO COBURN   )
)
         Plaintiff   )
)   Civil Action No. 00-386 JDS
)
vs.   )
)   Judge: John Dell Small, Jr.
WALLY MARTINEZ   )
)
         Defendant   )

SCHEDULING STIPULATION

The parties to this action, through their undersigned counsel, hereby stipulate and

agree as follows:

1. Defendant shall have until May 14, YR-00, to serve and file motions pursuant to

Rule 12 of the Federal Rules of Civil Procedure;

[Document page 1]

2. Plaintiff shall have until May 24, YR-00, to respond to Defendant's Rule 12 motions.

3. Unless Defendant's Rule 12 motions result in the dismissal of this action in its entirety, Defendant shall serve and file an answer to the complaint within ten days after notice of the court's action on Defendant's Rule 12 motions.

4. The hearing on Plaintiff's Motion for a Preliminary Injunction shall be continued from the previously scheduled date of April 20, YR-00, at 9:30 a.m., until June 27, YR-00, at 9:00 a.m. Both parties request an evidentiary hearing.

5. The Temporary Restraining Order entered on April 10, YR-00, shall be extended pursuant to Fed. R. Civ. P. 65 until the dismissal of this action or the disposition of Plaintiff's motion for a preliminary injunction, whichever first occurs, and Defendant hereby waives any right to appeal from the Temporary Restraining Order by virtue of its being extended.

Dated: April 19, YR-00

Respectfully submitted,

Elizabeth Ford   *Dean Manning*

Elizabeth Ford   Dean Manning

Ford & Burns   Manning & Kobalewski
Phelps Building   3875 Trupers Pike, Suite 211
233 Dodge Street   Dewey City, New York 13213
Dewey City, New York 13213   Telephone (891) 777-6563
Telephone: (891) 776-5400

              Attorney for Defendant,
Attorney for Plaintiff,   Wally Martinez
Mary Jo Coburn

Approved. It is so ordered.

John Dell Small, Jr., U.S.D.J.

[Document page 3]

Manning & Kobalewski
3875 Trupers Pike, Suite 211
Dewey City, New York 13213
Telephone (891) 777-6563

Dean Manning
Attorney for Defendant,
Wally Martinez

In the
UNITED STATES DISTRICT COURT
FOR THE CENTRAL DISTRICT OF NEW YORK

MARY JO COBURN	)	
	)	
Plaintiff	)	
	)	Civil Action No. 00-386 JDS
vs.	)	
	)	Judge: John Dell Small, Jr.
WALLY MARTINEZ	)	
	)	
Defendant	)	

MOTION TO DISMISS THE COMPLAINT FOR FAILURE TO STATE A CLAIM UPON WHICH RELIEF CAN BE GRANTED

The defendant, Wally Martinez, through undersigned counsel, hereby moves the court, pursuant to Rule 12(b)(6) of the Federal Rules of Civil Procedure, to dismiss this action for failure to state a claim upon which relief can be granted. As grounds for this motion, the defendant states as follows:

[Document page 1]

1. The law of Tennessee governs this action, and the purported cause of action on which plaintiff seeks relief is not recognized by the law of Tennessee. A Tennessee court would dismiss the complaint in this action if this action had been brought in Tennessee. Therefore, this court, applying, as it must, the law of Tennessee, should dismiss this action.

   a. Plaintiff was born in Tennessee, grew up in Tennessee, and has resided and taught school in Tennessee for the past five years; all of Plaintiff's close friends and relatives also reside in Tennessee; Plaintiff is currently seeking employment as a police officer in Tennessee; the alleged tort on which plaintiff sues was committed (if it was committed at all) in Tennessee; and all of the damage that plaintiff alleges to be the result of defendant's conduct as alleged in the complaint has occurred (if it has occurred at all) and will occur (if it will occur at all) within the State of Tennessee.

   b. New York has no interest in the outcome of this action seeking relief on behalf of a resident of Tennessee.

2. Even if this action is governed by New York law, the court should still dismiss Count Three of the complaint for failure to state a claim upon which relief can be granted. New York law does not impose liability for breach of a fiduciary duty of confidentiality upon one who does not induce the breach or

[Document page 2]

act in concert with the primary violator, even if the defendant knows of the breach and accepts benefits resulting therefrom.

Wherefore, the Defendant, Wally Martinez, respectfully submits that this action should be dismissed in its entirety for failure to state a claim upon which relief can be granted or, in the alternative, that Count Three of the complaint should be dismissed for failure to state a claim upon which relief can be granted.

Dated: May 14, YR-00

Respectfully submitted,

Dean Manning

Dean Manning

Manning & Kobalewski
3875 Trupers Pike, Suite 211
Dewey City, New York 13213
Telephone (891) 777-6563

Dean Manning
Attorney for the Defendant,
Wally Martinez

CERTIFICATE OF SERVICE

I certify that on this 14th day of May, YR-00, I served the foregoing

Motion to Dismiss the Complaint for Failure to State a Claim upon Which

Relief Can Be Granted upon the Plaintiff, Mary Jo Coburn, by causing a copy

thereof to be mailed, first class postage prepaid, to her attorney of record,

Elizabeth Ford, Ford & Burns, Phelps Building, 233 Dodge Street, Dewey

City, New York 13213.

Dean Manning
_____
Dean Manning

Manning & Kobalewski
3875 Trupers Pike, Suite 211
Dewey City, New York 13213
Telephone (891) 777-6563

Dean Manning
Attorney for the Defendant,
Wally Martinez

Manning & Kobalewski
3875 Trupers Pike, Suite 211
Dewey City, New York 13213
Telephone (891) 777-6563

Dean Manning
Attorney for Defendant,
Wally Martinez

UNITED STATES DISTRICT COURT
FILED
June 14, YR-00
CENTRAL DISTRICT OF NEW YORK

In the
UNITED STATES DISTRICT COURT
FOR THE CENTRAL DISTRICT OF NEW YORK

MARY JO COBURN	)	
	)	
Plaintiff	)	
	)	Civil Action No. 00-386 JDS
vs.	)	
	)	Judge: John Dell Small, Jr.
WALLY MARTINEZ	)	
	)	
Defendant	)	

ANSWER

1. Defendant admits paragraph 1 of the complaint.

2. Defendant is without knowledge or information sufficient to form a belief as to the truth of paragraphs 2-7 of the complaint.

8. Defendant admits that on or about April 2, YR-00, he obtained copies of one or more tape recordings, which were represented as being of a

conversation between Plaintiff and another person, and otherwise Defendant denies the allegations of paragraph 8 of the complaint.

9. Defendant denies the allegations of paragraph 9 of the complaint.

10. Defendant is without knowledge or information sufficient to form a belief as to the truth of paragraph 10 of the complaint.

11. Defendant is considering whether to upload the contents of the tapes onto his Web site, www.outlawcops.com, and otherwise Defendant denies the allegations of paragraph 11 of the complaint.

12. Except for the reference to threats, which Defendant denies, Defendant admits paragraph 12 of the complaint

13. Defendant denies paragraphs 13-19 of the complaint.

<u>FIRST DEFENSE</u>

The tape recordings referred to in the complaint contain newsworthy information that is of great public interest in that they concern a police shooting in Dewey City, New York, and subsequent investigation of the shooting by the Dewey City Police Department and the Dewey County District Attorney, which shooting and investigation were the subject of extensive press coverage and raise substantial questions as to the training and supervision of police officers in Dewey City, as to the efficiency and integrity of the entire command structure of the Dewey City Police Department and the Dewey County District Attorney's Office, as to the accuracy and integrity of investigations by public officials in Dewey City, and

[Document page 2]

as to the character and fitness of an individual who has applied for appointment as a police patrol officer in New Taft, Tennessee, and who, if appointed and authorized to carry a firearm, may be a clear and present danger to the public. Accordingly, publication of the said tape recordings would be justified by the public interest and would not be unlawful under the law of either New York or Tennessee, which governs this action.

SECOND DEFENSE

Defendant here incorporates by reference the allegations of the FIRST DEFENSE. Defendant's publication of the tape recordings described in the complaint is protected by the First Amendment to the United States Constitution, and any injunction against such publication would be an unlawful prior restraint in violation of the First Amendment.

Dated: June 14, YR-00

Respectfully submitted,

Dean Manning
_____

Manning & Kobalewski
3875 Trupers Pike, Suite 211
Dewey City, New York 13213
Telephone (891) 777-6563

Dean Manning
Attorney for the Defendant,
Wally Martinez

[Document page 3]

CERTIFICATE OF SERVICE

I certify that on this 14th day of June, YR-00, I served the foregoing Answer upon the Plaintiff, Mary Jo Coburn, by causing a copy thereof to be mailed, first class postage prepaid, to her attorney of record, Elizabeth Ford, Ford & Burns, Phelps Building, 233 Dodge Street, Dewey City, New York 13213.

Dean Manning

Dean Manning

Manning & Kobalewski
3875 Trupers Pike, Suite 211
Dewey City, New York 13213
Telephone (891) 777-6563

Dean Manning
Attorney for the Defendant,
Wally Martinez

[Document page 4]

UNITED STATES DISTRICT COURT
FOR THE CENTRAL DISTRICT OF NEW YORK

```
MARY JO COBURN          )
                        )
    Plaintiff           )
                        )
  vs.                   )     Civil Action No. 00-386 JDS
                        )
WALLY MARTINEZ          )
                        )
    Defendant           )
```

TRANSCRIPT OF PROCEEDINGS

BE IT REMEMBERED that the above captioned matter came on for a hearing on Plaintiff's Motion for a Preliminary Injunction this 27th day of June, YR-00, at 9:00 a.m., in Courtroom B-12, Old Post Office Building, 607 Victoria Street, Dewey City, New York, THE HONORABLE JOHN DELL SMALL, JR., presiding.

APPEARANCES:

    Elizabeth Ford
       For the Plaintiff, Mary Jo Coburn

    Dean Manning
       For the Defendant, Wally Martinez

* * * * *

[Document page 1]

1   THE COURT: Good morning. In case number 00-386, Coburn

2   versus Martinez, the court will now hear plaintiff's motion

3   for a preliminary injunction. The court has reviewed all the

4   papers previously filed in this matter and is thoroughly

5   familiar with the record and the issues presented. The

6   parties have requested an evidentiary hearing. Ms. Ford,

7   you may call your first witness.

8   MS. FORD: Good morning, Your Honor. Thank you. Plaintiff

9   calls Mary Jo Coburn.

10   TESTIMONY OF MARY JO COBURN

11   WITNESS SWORN

12   DIRECT EXAMINATION BY MS. FORD:

13   Q   Good morning, Ms. Coburn. Would you please state your

14   name for the record and spell your last name?

15   A   Mary Jo Coburn. C-O-B-U-R-N.

16   Q   Ms. Coburn, you are the plaintiff in this action?

17   A   Yes, I am.

18   Q   Would you briefly describe your background before you

19   first came to Dewey City.

20   THE COURT: This is covered in her declaration for the TRO.

21   MS. FORD: Yes, Your Honor. I thought it would be helpful if

22   Ms. Coburn described the events leading up to this

23   litigation in order —

[Document page 2]

1   THE COURT: In the interests of time, would there be any

2   objection to your simply entering Ms. Coburn's declaration

3   into evidence, having her swear to its truth, you ask

4   whatever additional questions you need, and then tender the

5   witness for cross-examination?

6   MS. FORD: If Your Honor prefers to proceed that way, I

7   certainly have no objection as long as Mr. Manning is

8   agreeable.

9   MR. MANNING: We have no objection to Ms. Coburn's testimony

10   being tendered in written form. However, we do object to

11   those portions of her declaration in which she describes

12   conversations with others. In particular her conversations

13   with Dr. Plano. Those we object to as hearsay.

14   THE COURT: Ms. Ford?

15   MS. FORD: We will be calling Dr. Plano as a witness, so I

16   don't see what the problem is.

17   THE COURT: Why don't you go ahead as the court suggested and

18   we will rule on particular objections as they arise.

19   BY MS. FORD:

20   Q   Referring the court and counsel to the document that has

21   previously been marked as Plaintiff's Exhibit # 1 for

22   identification, Ms. Coburn, I show you Plaintiff's

23   Exhibit # 1 for identification and ask if you recognize

[Document page 3]

1   it?

2 A   Yes. It is the declaration that I signed just before

3   bringing this lawsuit.

4 Q   Have you recently reviewed that declaration?

5 A   Yes, I have.

6 Q   Are all the statements that you made in that declaration

7   the truth?

8 A   Yes.

9 MS. FORD: Plaintiff offers in evidence Plaintiff's Exhibit #

10 1 entitled Declaration of Mary Jo Coburn in Support of

11 Plaintiff's Motion for a Temporary Restraining Order,

12 previously filed in this action on April 10, YR-00.

13 MR. MANNING: We object to the following passages as hearsay.

14 The third and fourth sentences of paragraph 5. The third

15 sentence of paragraph 7 is not based on the personal

16 knowledge of the witness. All of paragraph 13 after the

17 second sentence is hearsay, all about what Dr. Plano told

18 her. The same for paragraph 14 and also paragraph 15 and 16

19 and 17. It's all hearsay. Also we object to paragraph 20

20 as speculative and not based on personal knowledge.

21 THE COURT: The hearsay objections will be overruled. All

22 these statements are admissible to show Ms. Coburn's state

23 of mind. I read paragraph 7 as the witness speaking of her

1   own experience and what is well known to her. She is not

2   going beyond her personal knowledge. So that's overruled.

3   As for paragraph 20, most of it describes the witness's own

4   actions. The last sentence describes Mr. Martinez's

5   intentions, but that seems to be rationally based on the

6   witness's own perceptions. So that objection will be

7   overruled as well. Ms. Coburn's declaration will be

8   received. You are certainly at liberty to cross-examine her

9   about it.

10   (PLAINTIFF'S EXHIBIT # 1 RECEIVED IN EVIDENCE.)

11   MS. FORD: I have no further questions of this witness at

12   this time.

13   THE COURT: Mr. Manning?

14   CROSS-EXAMINATION BY MR. MANNING:

15   Q   On January 13, YR-06, while on duty as a police patrol

16   officer in this city, you shot and killed Ubumu

17   Victoire, correct?

18   A   Yes. He was threatening my life.

19   Q   Mr. Victoire had been turned over to you by other

20   officers who had arrested him, right?

21   A   Yes.

22   Q   You had never seen him before, correct?

23   A   Correct.

[Document page 5]

1   Q   As a matter of fact, Officer Coburn, you became

2   acquainted with Ubumu Victoire long before January 13,

3   YR-06, didn't you?

4   MS. FORD: Objection. That's totally irrelevant to this

5   case. In fact, this entire line of questioning is

6   irrelevant and I move to strike it.

7   THE COURT: The objection is sustained. The motion to strike

8   is overruled. No harm was done. Next question, please,

9   counsel.

10   BY MR. MANNING:

11   Q   As a matter of fact, you and Mr. Victoire had become

12   very close friends when he was on the criminal justice

13   faculty at —

14   MS. FORD: Your Honor, this is totally uncalled for. You

15   have already ruled that —

16   THE COURT: Yes. Mr. Manning, I would suggest you move onto

17   some subject that is relevant. We are not here to retry the

18   issue of Mr. Victoire's death.

19   BY MR. MANNING:

20   Q   In paragraph 5 of your declaration, you have no factual

21   basis for characterizing the District Attorney's

22   investigation as thorough, do you?

23   MS. FORD: Objection.   Irrelevant.

[Document page 6]

1   THE COURT: Mr. Manning, how does this relate?

2   MR. MANNING: Your Honor, these tapes are newsworthy tapes

3   and they concern a matter of great public interest. Ms.

4   Coburn, who used her police service revolver to shoot Mr.

5   Victoire in the back, has never given a public accounting of

6   herself. She hides behind the screen of so-called

7   exoneration by the D.A.'s office and the police department,

8   claiming innocence because of their thorough investigation.

9   Well, I would like to have her tell us just how thorough

10   they were.

11   THE COURT: The objection is overruled.

12   BY MR. MANNING:

13   Q   Just how thorough was the D.A.'s investigation that you

14   claim to have exonerated you?

15   A   I don't know. They interviewed me very extensively. I

16   know they ran ballistics tests. Other than that I don't

17   know. They told me it was a thorough investigation, but

18   I don't know.

19   MR. MANNING: Move to strike the last statement as hearsay.

20   THE COURT: Granted. The court will ignore that part of the

21   testimony.

22   BY MR. MANNING:

23   Q   For all you know, the D.A.'s investigation was routine

[Document page 7]

1   and perfunctory?

2   A   I guess so.

3   Q   And the same goes for the Internal Affairs Division

4   investigation, doesn't it?

5   A   I really don't know.

6   Q   Referring to paragraph 7 of your declaration, you refer

7   to childhood traumas, fears, dreams, and that sort of

8   thing. Did you discuss your childhood traumas, fears,

9   and dreams with Dr. Plano?

10   MS. FORD: Objection. That's privileged. In the sentence just

11   before, Ms. Coburn states that what she said in her sessions

12   with Dr. Plano is nobody's business, and that is the truth.

13   If necessary to vindicate the doctor-patient privilege, I

14   will instruct my client not to answer any questions about

15   her therapeutic communications with Dr. Plano.

16   THE COURT: Mr. Manning, the objection is well taken. The

17   court will not allow you to intrude upon privileged

18   communications in order to vindicate your claim to publish

19   the privileged communications that are on those tapes. You

20   will have to do it some other way.

21   MR. MANNING: Yes, Your Honor. Further along in paragraph 7,

22   Ms. Coburn states that she had no choice and she did the

23   right thing as a police officer when she shot Mr. Victoire.

[Document page 8]

1   Based on Your Honor's rulings, I assume that if I try to

2   examine her about that statement Your Honor would probably

3   rule the inquiry to be irrelevant. Therefore, I would like

4   to move to strike that sentence from the declaration on

5   grounds of irrelevancy.

6   THE COURT: The sentence is in there to explain her reasons

7   for needing psychotherapy. She speaks of her belief. Her

8   reasons for needing psychotherapy are useful background

9   information, but they are only tangentially relevant. I'm

10   going to let it stand. I would suggest that you move on to

11   your next line of inquiry.

12   BY MR. MANNING:

13   Q   In paragraph 11 you speak of flashbacks. Have you had

14   any flashbacks since October 3, YR-04?

15   A   A few.

16   Q   How many?

17   A   I'm not sure.

18   Q   When is the last time you had a flashback?

19   A   Maybe two, three years ago.

20   Q   So your therapy with Dr. Plano did not cure you of

21   flashbacks?

22   A   Not entirely. But it helped a lot.

23   Q   If you were to be hired as a police officer in New Taft,

[Document page 9]

1   Tennessee, there's really nothing that keeps you from

2   having another flashback while on duty as a police

3   officer and while you are armed with a fully loaded and

4   operational revolver, is there? The same kind of

5   revolver you used to shoot Ubumu Victoire in the back,

6   is there?

7   MS. FORD: Objection. Argumentative. He's badgering the

8   witness.

9   THE COURT: Would you please rephrase the question to remove

10   some of the histrionics, Mr. Manning?

11   MR. MANNING: Yes, Your Honor.

12   BY MR. MANNING:

13   Q   There's nothing in particular to guarantee that you will

14   not have a flashback at some future time while on duty

15   as a police officer in New Taft, Tennessee, is there?

16   A   There aren't many guarantees in this life. But I don't

17   think there's any danger along the lines you are

18   suggesting.

19   Q   Well, if someone wanted to evaluate the danger in your

20   particular case, it sure would help if they could listen

21   to what you had to say on those tapes, wouldn't it?

22   A   You mean what I said to my psychiatrist behind closed

23   doors?

[Document page 10]

1   Q   Yes.

2   MS. FORD: If Your Honor please, you were very clear in our

3   conference this morning that Mr. Manning was not going to be

4   allowed to wheedle out the contents of the tapes. The last

5   question is getting pretty close, don't you think?

6   THE COURT: I will allow the question. Ms. Coburn, the

7   question does not ask you to reveal anything that was said.

8   It only asks for your opinion as to the usefulness of the

9   tapes in evaluating your fitness to serve as a police

10   officer. Do you understand the question?

11   THE WITNESS: I think I do.

12   THE COURT: What is your answer?

13   THE WITNESS: My answer is that I don't know.

14   BY MR. MANNING:

15   Q   Referring to paragraph 14, your conversation with Dr.

16   Plano, do you have any independent information as to

17   what, if anything, was said between Dr. Plano and the

18   so-called anonymous caller?

19   A   No.

20   Q   And the same would be true of whatever was said between

21   Dr. Plano and the records management company?

22   A   Right.

23   Q   In paragraph 18, you say you received phone calls from,

[Document page 11]

1 I quote, a man purporting to be Dr. Plano's anonymous

2 caller. What exactly did the man say? He didn't say,

3 "I am Dr. Plano's anonymous caller," did he?

4 A No. I remember he said, "I am the man you have been

5 waiting to hear from." I just figured he was referring

6 to the person that had been calling Dr. Plano.

7 Q Did he mention Dr. Plano's name?

8 A No.

9 Q Did he say anything about an anonymous caller?

10 A Not that I recall.

11 Q Referring to paragraph 19, Mr. Martinez never spoke of

12 your psychotherapy sessions with Dr. Plano, did he —

13 that is, he never used the name of Dr. Plano in talking

14 about your psychotherapy sessions, did he?

15 A I don't think so. I may have mentioned her name, but I

16 don't think he did.

17 Q And he didn't tell you how he came by the tapes, did he?

18 A He said he had bought them from a guy who had gotten the

19 tapes legitimately, and that it was all legal and

20 aboveboard. Which of course was a lie. There's no way

21 anyone except for the doctor and myself could legally

22 get hold of those tapes.

23 Q Have you attended law school?

[Document page 12]

1   A   No.

2   MR. MANNING: I move to strike the last part of the witness's

3   previous answer about nobody could legally get hold of the

4   tapes. It's a legal opinion and she is not qualified to give

5   a legal opinion.

6   THE COURT: The testimony may stand. The court understood

7   the witness to be expressing her understanding that the

8   tapes were confidential. It's not a big deal. Next

9   question.

10   BY MR. MANNING:

11   Q   At any time during your telephone conversations with Mr.

12   Martinez, did he explicitly mention Dr. Plano's name?

13   A   Not that I recall.

14   Q   Did he in any way indicate that he thought these tapes

15   had been leaked by Dr. Plano?

16   A   No.

17   Q   Did he in any way indicate that he was aware that these

18   tapes were legally confidential communications between a

19   doctor and a patient?

20   A   Well, he never said anything like that. But he had to

21   know because I told him as much.

22   Q   What did you tell him?

23   A   I told him that if he had the tapes I thought he did,

1   then he had no right to them because they were part of

2   my confidential medical records and they were protected

3   by law.

4   Q   He never said that he agreed with your characterization,

5   did he?

6   A   No, but he obviously knew what was going on.

7   MR. MANNING: Move to strike the last answer as unresponsive

8   and based on speculation.

9   THE COURT: Motion granted. The court will disregard the

10   last answer.

11   BY MR. MANNING:

12   Q   Now, Ms. Coburn, in paragraph 20 you say you offered to

13   help Mr. Martinez locate documentary evidence about the

14   investigation into the death of Mr. Victoire. Did you

15   make such an offer?

16   A   Yes.

17   Q   And did you in fact have access to documentary evidence

18   into the death of Mr. Victoire?

19   MS. FORD: Your Honor, I believe that Ms. Coburn should be

20   advised of her rights as to the last question.

21   THE COURT: I assume that you have done so.

22   MS. FORD: If I may, Your Honor, I would advise Ms. Coburn to

23   listen carefully before attempting to answer it.

[Document page 14]

1   THE COURT: Ms. Coburn, do you understand what is going on

2   here?

3   THE WITNESS: I think so. I don't think I should answer the

4   last question because the answer I would give might tend to

5   incriminate me.

6   THE COURT: The court will uphold your claim of privilege.

7   You are not required to answer the last question. What is

8   your next question, Mr. Manning?

9   BY MR. MANNING:

10   Q   In paragraphs 21 through 23, you speak of your

11   embarrassment if the tapes should be revealed. There is

12   nothing embarrassing about a police officer honestly and

13   properly carrying out her sworn duty, is there?

14   MS. FORD: Objection. Mr. Manning is attempting to do

15   indirectly what Your Honor has forbidden. The question is

16   seeking to reveal the contents of the tapes. He can't do

17   that.

18   THE COURT: Mr. Manning, unless you can state a legitimate

19   purpose for your last question I must sustain the objection.

20   MR. MANNING: I withdraw the question.

21   BY MR. MANNING:

22   Q   Do you currently have any close friends or family in New

23   York State?

[Document page 15]

1   A   No.

2   Q   Any former colleagues on the Dewey City Police

3   Department that you keep in touch with?

4   A   No.

5   Q   Any friends from college?

6   A   There's one.

7   Q   Where does she live? Am I right in calling your friend

8   she?

9   A   She lives in Vermont.

10   Q   Any college friends that live in New York State?

11   A   I suppose some do, but I don't keep up with any of them.

12   Q   Are you concerned about your reputation among peace

13   officers and criminal justice professionals?

14   A   To some extent.

15   Q   Are you concerned about your reputation in Tennessee?

16   A   To some extent.

17   Q   Are you concerned about your professional reputation

18   anywhere outside Tennessee?

19   A   Not really. Tennessee is my home. That's where I want

20   to stay.

21   Q   So would it be correct to say that all the damages and

22   injuries you allege in your complaint have occurred or

23   will occur within the State of Tennessee.

[Document page 16]

```
 1    A    I guess so. Only when I say I have been very upset by

 2         Mr. Martinez's threat to publish my confidential medical

 3         records, I am upset wherever I happen to be. I am

 4         suffering from his actions this very moment, here in

 5         this courtroom in New York.

 6    Q    You don't plan to stay in New York after this hearing is

 7         over, do you?

 8    A    No.

 9    Q    You will return to your full-time residence in

10         Tennessee, right?

11    A    Right.

12    Q    And it is also correct to say that all of the so-called

13         threats that you have received from Mr. Martinez have

14         been received by you in New Taft, Tennessee. Isn't that

15         right?

16    A    Well, he hasn't threatened me since I arrived in Dewey

17         City for this hearing, if that's what you mean.

18    Q    The only so-called threats that Mr. Martinez has made

19         were by telephone, correct?

20    A    That's right.

21    Q    And you were in Tennessee for all of those phone calls,

22         right?

23    A    Yes.
```

[Document page 17]

1　　MR. MANNING: No further questions.

2　　THE COURT: Any redirect?

3　　MS. FORD: No, Your Honor.

4　　THE COURT: The witness may step down.

5　　MS. FORD: Plaintiff calls Dr. Christal Plano.

6　　　　　　　　　　TESTIMONY OF CHRISTAL PLANO, M.D.

7　　WITNESS SWORN

8　　DIRECT EXAMINATION BY MS. FORD:

9　　Q　Good morning. Would you please state your full name and

10　　　　then spell your name for the record?

11　　A　Yes. Good morning. My name is Christal Plano. Christal

12　　　　is spelled C-H-R-I-S-T-A-L and Plano is P-L-A-N-O.

13　　Q　Thank you. Dr. Plano, would you please describe your

14　　　　educational and professional background?

15　　A　Yes. My undergraduate degree was from Cornell in YR-35.

16　　　　I earned my M.D. at Johns Hopkins University. My

17　　　　internship was at Hahnemann Hospital in Philadelphia.

18　　　　After that I completed residencies in psychiatry and

19　　　　neurology at the University of Washington Hospital in

20　　　　Seattle and Massachusetts General Hospital in Boston. I

21　　　　am board certified in both psychiatry and neurology. I

22　　　　am licensed to practice medicine by the State of New

23　　　　York. I have been practicing psychiatry in Dewey City,

[Document page 18]

1   New York, since YR-17.

2   Q   You are here today under subpoena?

3   A   Yes.

4   Q   You understand that, while you are being called as a

5   witness on behalf of your former patient, Mary Jo

6   Coburn, Ms. Coburn does not consent to your revealing

7   any of her confidential communications with you as your

8   patient or your confidential communications with her as

9   her psychiatrist? If any question threatens to reveal

10   any confidential or privileged communications between

11   you and Ms. Coburn, you are to call attention to that

12   fact and must refuse to answer the question. Is that

13   clear?

14   A   Yes.

15   Q   During what period of time was Ms. Coburn your patient?

16   A   She began psychotherapy with me in the summer of YR-06.

17   She terminated in March YR-05. Then she returned for

18   brief follow-up treatment in September YR-04.

19   Q   Do you recall the dates on which she saw you for follow-

20   up treatment?

21   A   Yes. We had a total of three sessions on September

22   20th, September 27th, and the last one was September

23   29th.

[Document page 19]

1   Q   Going back to the beginning of her therapy, how is it

2   that you came to tape-record her sessions?

3   A   It is a routine I follow with all my patients. It is

4   how I was trained, although not many psychiatrists use

5   this technique anymore. The point is to have a detailed

6   and accurate record of every therapy session without the

7   distraction of taking notes. I can listen intently and

8   interact freely with the patient and still be able to

9   review each session in great detail if need be. I

10   always explain the purpose to the patient and get

11   informed consent. The tapes are part of each patient's

12   medical file.

13   Q   And that is the practice that you followed with Ms.

14   Coburn?

15   A   Yes.

16   Q   Did you record every session?

17   A   Yes.

18   Q   How and where did you keep the tapes?

19   A   I have a file cabinet for tape cassettes. It is as

20   secure as a regular file cabinet and is kept in my

21   office file room. When a patient is no longer active, I

22   send the medical records, including the tapes, to a

23   records management company, where they are kept.

1   Q   What records management company do you use?

2   A   Gibraltar, here in Dewey City.

3   Q   Have you ever had any problem with Gibraltar failing to

4   keep your patient's records safely and securely or

5   letting them fall into the wrong hands?

6   A   Never.

7   Q   Did you cause the tapes of some of Ms. Coburn's

8   psychotherapy sessions to be delivered to Mr. Wally

9   Martinez?

10   A   Regrettably, yes.

11   Q   How did that happen?

12   A   Ms. Coburn had been an extremely difficult patient. I

13   can't get into why, except to say that I experienced a

14   great deal of frustration as her therapist. I last saw

15   her, as I said, in September YR-04, and then out of the

16   blue I get a phone call from her nearly four years

17   later. She said she had applied for a police job in New

18   Taft, Tennessee.

19   Q   Do you remember the date she called you?

20   A   It was March 15, YR-00. She called me in the early

21   afternoon. She said she had applied for a police job

22   and needed a letter from me. My immediate thought was,

23   "My God, how can this woman possibly want to be a cop

1   again?   After all she has been through." While I had not

2   seen her for some years, the sound of her voice on the

3   phone flooded my mind with unpleasant and conflicted

4   memories. I remembered — Well, I shouldn't go into that.

5   I can just say that my mind and body were overcome with

6   an overwhelming feeling of fear, foreboding, and dread.

7   Q What did you tell her?

8   A I remember thinking that I should stall for time. I

9   needed to collect my thoughts. So I made up a line

10   about needing to review her file and a concern about her

11   waiving confidentiality. And so I told her that I would

12   have to order up her file, and I would get back to her

13   in a few days.

14 Q What happened next?

15 A I sought counsel from a few people whose advice I trust.

16   While they cautioned me against rash action and said

17   that all my concerns could be handled through proper

18   channels, at the same time I was decompensating very

19   badly at a personal level. I had never really resolved

20   my countertransference with Mary Jo. I was experiencing

21   considerable turmoil in my personal life at the time.

22   Then I relapsed rather badly into a drug problem that

23   has plagued me for much of my adult life. To make a

[Document page 22]

1   long story short, I totally lost control, fell into the

2   grip of a drug-induced paranoia and grandiosity, and

3   decided that it should be my mission to save the world

4   from Mary Jo Coburn. It would not do just to write a

5   negative letter of recommendation or to communicate on

6   the q.t. with the New Taft Police Department personnel

7   office. No, I convinced myself that I had to tell the

8   world about this dangerous demon that I had created in

9   my own mind. That's when I decided to use Mr. Wally

10   Martinez as the instrument for carrying out my grandiose

11   fantasy.

12 Q How did you know Mr. Martinez?

13 A I didn't know him. I knew of him. He was a newspaper

14   reporter who covered the Victoire shooting and the

15   investigations. It was obvious from his columns that he

16   had not been satisfied with the official outcomes, and

17   he had publicly propounded several unanswered questions

18   about the shooting and the investigation. I knew that

19   he had become like a crusader against police abuses and

20   brutality. So I figured that if anyone would be

21   interested in the straight scoop about Mary Jo it was

22   Wally Martinez.

23 Q Did you contact him?

[Document page 23]

1   A   Not directly. I wanted to splash the truth about Mary Jo

2   across newspapers, TV shows, and Web sites all around

3   the country. I figured Wally Martinez could do that.

4   But I also wanted to maintain complete deniability for

5   having anything to do with the leak. So I decided to

6   use an intermediary.

7   Q   Who was that?

8   A   His name is Forrest Klepperman. Not many people know

9   it, but Forrest is my brother. He is kind of the black

10   sheep of the family. He had been in trouble a long

11   while back, and I helped him get back on his feet by

12   landing him a job at Gibraltar Records Management.

13   That's the same place where I store my medical records.

14   There is a family connection. So Forrest had been

15   working at Gibraltar for about three years, and I knew

16   he knew his way around Gibraltar and would do whatever I

17   asked him. So I called him and told him to get out the

18   Mary Jo Coburn file and extract two particular cassette

19   tapes. He should make copies of those tapes, put the

20   file back, and then arrange to pass the tape copies on

21   to Wally Martinez. I knew that Martinez would

22   immediately recognize the explosive nature of these

23   tapes and would make a big deal of them. Without taking

[Document page 24]

1   it any further, I figured that the disclosure of these

2   tapes would make it certain that Mary Jo Coburn could

3   never again work as a police officer anywhere in the

4   United States.

5   Q   You say there were two particular cassette tapes that

6   you directed Mr. Klepperman to. Which were they?

7   A   Our sessions in September, YR-04.

8   Q   So what happened after you told Forrest to get those

9   tapes and copy them?

10 A   I am not entirely sure. I told Forrest what I needed

11   him to do, and I also told him that I needed to stay

12   hidden in the background. But as far as I can tell, as

13   soon as Martinez expressed doubts about whether these

14   tapes were genuine, Forrest brought my name into it, and

15   the next thing I knew I got a phone call from Martinez

16   saying he had these tapes and could I authenticate them.

17 Q   When did you receive that call?

18 A   March 28th.

19 Q   How did you respond to Mr. Martinez's request?

20 A   I was already beginning to get cold feet at that point,

21   so I put him off. I basically let him know that what he

22   had was the genuine article. He knew that Mary Jo had

23   suffered from posttraumatic stress syndrome after the

[Document page 25]

1   Victoire affair, and he knew that she had seen me for

2   therapy. He put two and two together and figured that I

3   was trying to blow the whistle on her. He did not press

4   me too hard. But when I gave him Mary Jo's number to

5   call, he went right after her.

6   Q   Was that in the same telephone conversation?

7   A   No, that was later.

8   Q   When?

9   A   I believe it was on April 2nd.

10   Q   How did you come to give him Mary Jo's number?

11   A   Well, after Martinez called me and was playing me these

12   tape excerpts and asking if I could verify them, I began

13   to get feelings of remorse about what I had done. In

14   fact, I asked Martinez if he would let me have the tapes

15   back, but he wouldn't do that. So I decided that the

16   best thing I could do to improve this terrible situation

17   that I had created was to warn Mary Jo. So I called her

18   and told her what had happened.

19   Q   When did you call her?

20   A   It was on March 28th.

21   Q   Of this year?

22   A   Yes.

23   Q   What did you say to her?

[Document page 26]

1   A   I told her that there had been a leak from Gibraltar and

2   that someone had called me anonymously to try to

3   authenticate some tapes that sounded like hers.

4   Eventually she asked me to put her in touch with this

5   caller, and so I got her OK to give Martinez her phone

6   number. That's about all I know until I got wind that

7   Mary Jo had sued Wally Martinez, and then I got your

8   subpoena to come to court. I could try to lie and cover

9   up my part, but I feel quite badly about what I did, and

10   I have decided that however it turns out I need to tell

11   the truth about my part and hope for the best.

12   Q   When did Ms. Coburn tell you it would be OK to give Mr.

13   Martinez her phone number?

14   A   She called me on March 30th and said she wanted to talk

15   directly to the guy who had her tapes and could I tell

16   her how to reach him. I told her I didn't know, but

17   when he called back I would ask him to call her. And she

18   told me to go ahead and give him her number so he could

19   call her. I am not sure exactly what she had in mind,

20   but I knew she had already consulted a lawyer and I

21   figured she knew what she was doing.

22   Q   When you arranged for Mr. Klepperman to deliver these

23   tapes to Mr. Martinez, was it your intention that Mr.

[Document page 27]

1   Martinez should publish them?

2 A At that time, yes. Later I realized how wrong I was.

3 Q Couldn't you have published them without his help?

4 A Yes and no. I certainly did not have my own access to

5   communications media. I needed a journalist helper.

6   Martinez was the one who came to mind because of his

7   previous connection to the case.

8 Q To what extent was Mr. Martinez aware that the tapes

9   were of confidential sessions between a psychiatrist and

10   a patient?

11 A I hardly know, but he would have to be a complete idiot

12   not to get it.

13 Q To what extent was Mr. Martinez aware that he had come

14   into possession of these tapes because Ms. Coburn's

15   psychiatrist had decided to breach Ms. Coburn's

16   confidences in order to prevent her from reentering

17   police work?

18 A I think that was implicit in the situation. I don't

19   know exactly what he knew.

20 Q Do you have an opinion as to Ms. Coburn's fitness for

21   police work? Please just answer yes or no.

22 A I did at one time.

23 Q Can you testify about your opinion as to her fitness

1   without revealing any confidential communications

2   between you and Ms.Coburn?

3 A Only to a very limited extent. I can say that in YR-04

4   I had a very strong opinion, and it was negative. I can

5   also say that I have had no contact with Mary Jo since

6   that time, and people can change dramatically over the

7   course of four years. I am impressed by what I have

8   learned about her activities in the last few years. At

9   this point, I would have to say that I have no basis for

10   an opinion one way or the other about her current

11   fitness for police work.

12 MS. FORD: Thank you, Dr. Plano. No further questions.

13 CROSS-EXAMINATION BY MR. MANNING:

14 Q In the course of your work as a psychiatrist and

15   neurologist, you are sometimes called upon to evaluate

16   the fitness of an individual for a particular line of

17   work?

18 A Yes.

19 Q And do you regard yourself as qualified to perform that

20   sort of evaluation?

21 A Yes, to the extent that anyone is. There is a lot about

22   human behavior that we do not understand. And when

23   trained psychiatrists are asked in controlled settings

[Document page 29]

1   to make estimates of the likelihood that particular

2   individuals will in the future engage in violent acts,

3   their predictive power is not much better than chance.

4   Q   Have you been asked to evaluate the mental and emotional

5   fitness of individuals to serve as police officers?

6   A   Yes.

7   Q   You recognize, do you not, that police work is sensitive

8   and dangerous work, and that there is a huge and

9   legitimate public interest in ensuring that police

10   officers can handle themselves appropriately in the face

11   of danger?

12   A.   Absolutely.

13   Q   If you were called upon to evaluate the emotional and

14   mental fitness of an individual to serve as an armed

15   police officer, and you were informed that there was a

16   tape recording of that individual's session with her

17   psychiatrist whose contents were similar to the contents

18   of the tape recordings that you caused to be delivered

19   to Mr. Martinez, would you not think that the contents

20   of that tape recording were extremely pertinent to your

21   evaluation of the fitness of that individual to be a

22   cop?

23   MS. FORD: I object in that the question gets extremely close

[Document page 30]

1   to asking Dr. Plano to reveal the contents of the tapes.

2   THE COURT: I don't think so. I will allow it.

3   THE WITNESS: The answer to the question is yes.

4   BY MR. MANNING:

5   Q   So, if the appropriate body to evaluate the public

6   interest in whether Ms. Coburn should ever again be

7   certified for a police officer position is the public

8   itself, you agree, do you not, that the public has a

9   high level of interest in hearing the contents of the

10   tapes involved in this litigation?

11   A   I think I would agree.

12   Q   When Ms. Coburn first consulted you, would you say she

13   was seriously disturbed?

14   A   Yes.

15   Q   When you last saw her in September YR-04, would you say

16   she was seriously disturbed?

17   MS. FORD: Just a minute. I may have been asleep at the

18   switch here. But this question and the last one really seek

19   to reveal confidential communications between Ms. Coburn and

20   Dr. Plano. If Dr. Plano has any opinion about Ms. Coburn's

21   mental health, it is because of what occurred in therapy,

22   including everything Ms. Coburn has said and done. And so I

23   object to both this and the previous question on grounds of

[Document page 31]

1   privilege and ask that the last answer be stricken.

2   MR. MANNING: If Your Honor please, failure to object

3   constitutes a waiver of the privilege to the extent of that

4   question.

5   THE COURT: Mr. Manning is correct. The court will overrule

6   your motion to strike the next to last question. As to the

7   last question, let me ask the doctor. Do you have any basis

8   for forming an opinion as to whether Ms. Coburn was

9   disturbed in September YR-04 other than — other than what

10 you learned in your psychotherapy sessions with her?

11 THE WITNESS: No.

12 THE COURT: What about her demeanor and appearance apart from

13 the things she said to you in psychotherapy?

14 THE WITNESS: It is all intertwined.

15 THE COURT: Mr. Manning, the objection to your last question

16 is sustained on grounds that its effect is to inquire into

17 privileged communications. The witness will not be allowed

18 to answer. Continue.

19 MR. MANNING: Is Your Honor allowing the answer about mental

20 disturbance when Dr. Plano first started seeing Ms. Coburn

21 to stand on the basis of waiver?

22 THE COURT: That is correct.

23 MR. MANNING: Well, it seems to me then that what we have

[Document page 32]

1   here is a voluntary disclosure of a substantial part of the

2   communication. As Your Honor knows, the holder of a

3   privilege is not allowed to disclose part of a communication

4   and withhold the rest. So I am going to ask Your Honor to

5   rule that plaintiff has waived the doctor-patient privilege

6   at least for purposes of the testimony of this witness.

7   MS. FORD: Your Honor —

8   THE COURT: Ms. Ford, I do not need to hear from you on this.

9   Mr. Manning, your request borders on being frivolous. Your

10   request for a ruling of waiver is overruled.

11   BY MR. MANNING:

12   Q   Dr. Plano, you spoke with Ms. Coburn in March of this

13   year?

14   A   Yes.

15   Q   She asked you for a letter of reference?

16   A   More or less.

17   Q   It had been nearly five years since you had seen her in

18   therapy?

19   A   Yes.

20   Q   Your telephone conversation with her in March was not a

21   privileged communication, was it? Was it a therapy

22   session?

23   A   No, it wasn't therapy.

1 Q   You weren't being asked for medical services?

2 A   No.

3 Q   On the basis of your telephone conversation with Ms.

4   Coburn, you formed the opinion that Ms. Coburn was so

5   mentally unstable and disturbed and it would be so

6   dangerous to allow her even to get close to a police

7   uniform that you could see no other course than to blow

8   the whistle on her as an outlaw cop, and that's why you

9   decided to let my client in on Ms. Coburn's therapy

10   sessions, because she was so mentally ill that it would

11   be dangerous to even consider her for a position in

12   police work?

13 MS. FORD: Objection. Compound question and argumentative.

14 THE COURT: Mr. Manning, can you break that down into bite-

15 size pieces?

16 BY MR. MANNING:

17 Q   When you talked with Ms. Coburn in March, you came to a

18   conclusion about her mental health, didn't you?

19 A   I guess I did.

20 Q   And your conclusion was that she was seriously

21   disturbed, correct?

22 A   Yes.

23 Q   And that she would be dangerous as a police officer?

[Document page 34]

1   A   That's right.

2   Q   And nothing has happened since that phone call to change

3   your conclusion?

4   A   Well, I have changed my mind. I don't think I have any

5   basis for expressing an opinion about Ms. Coburn's

6   mental health or probable future behavior. It's been

7   too long. One phone call is not an adequate basis for an

8   opinion.

9   Q   You would not have gone to all the risk and trouble of

10   trying to release those tapes unless you thought that

11   Ms. Coburn would be extremely dangerous as a police

12   officer, would you?

13 A   Probably not.

14 MR. MANNING:

15   Your witness.

16 REDIRECT EXAMINATION BY MS. FORD:

17 Q   Let's talk about your own mental health in March. You

18   mentioned a lot of stress. You mentioned a drug

19   problem. Were you yourself in any condition to be

20   forming reliable opinions about Ms. Coburn, who had been

21   such a difficult and challenging patient?

22 A   That's exactly my point. I went off half-cocked. I made

23   a serious mistake of judgment, for which I am deeply

[Document page 35]

1   sorry. I do not think it would be right or fair to draw

2   any conclusion about Ms. Coburn from my actions last

3   March.

4   Q   Mr. Manning asked you what role the tapes might play in

5   determining a person's fitness for work. Let's talk

6   about the other things that would be of interest in

7   assessing the emotional and mental fitness of a person

8   to serve as a police officer. Would a recent clinical

9   interview be important?

10   A   Of course.

11   Q   You have not done a recent clinical interview of Ms.

12   Coburn, have you?

13   A   No.

14   Q   How about the results of current psychological testing?

15   A   Some psychological testing panels can be very helpful.

16   Q   In determining fitness for police work?

17   A   Yes.

18   Q   You do not have access to current psychological testing

19   results for Ms. Coburn, do you?

20   A   No.

21   Q   How about reports and letters of recommendation from

22   recent and current employers?

23   A   Often very helpful. But I do not happen to have access

[Document page 36]

1   to that sort of information about Ms. Coburn.

2   Q   You say you have in the past evaluated individuals for

3   mental and emotional fitness for police work?

4   A   Yes.

5   Q   And you have been willing and able to perform meaningful

6   evaluations even without access to detailed information

7   about their psychotherapy communications?

8   A   I don't know if the situation has ever arisen.

9   Q   Pretend you never met Mary Jo Coburn but were assigned

10   to help determine her mental and emotional fitness for

11   police work. You could do that, couldn't you?

12   A   Yes.

13   Q   And in doing that, you would use all the tools we have

14   previously discussed. A clinical interview?

15   Psychological tests?

16   A   I would also want family, employment, and educational

17   history as well.

18   Q   Now, if you learned that there were tape recordings of

19   prior psychotherapy sessions, would you feel that you

20   would have to get hold of them in order to render a

21   helpful opinion?

22   A   I don't think so. I would not expect to have access to

23   such information, certainly not of a private patient.

[Document page 37]

1   Q   And you would not need it in order to make a competent

2   diagnosis, would you?

3   A   No.

4   Q   And if you wouldn't need it, there's no earthly reason

5   why the so-called public needs it either, is there?

6   A   I agree with you.

7   MS. FORD: No further questions.

8   MR. MANNING: Nothing further.

9   THE COURT: Very well.

10   MS. FORD: May the witness be excused?

11   THE COURT: Certainly. Dr. Plano, you are excused. The court

12   thanks you for your testimony. I think this would be a good

13   point for our mid-morning recess.

14   (COURT IN RECESS FROM 10:49 A.M. TO 11:10 A.M.)

15   THE COURT: Back on the record in Coburn versus Martinez. Ms.

16   Ford.

17   MS. FORD: Forrest Klepperman, please.

18   TESTIMONY OF FORREST KLEPPERMAN

19   WITNESS SWORN

20   DIRECT EXAMINATION BY MS. FORD:

21   Q   Please state your name for the record and spell your

22   last name.

23   A   Sure. Forrest Klepperman. K-L-E-P-P-E-R-M-A-N.

[Document page 38]

1   THE COURT REPORTER: How do you spell your first name?

2   THE WITNESS: F-O-R-R-E-S-T.

3   BY MS. FORD:

4   Q   Mr. Klepperman, where do you live?

5   A   Here in Dewey City.

6   Q   Where do you work?

7   A   At Gibraltar Records Management.

8   Q   How long have you worked there?

9   A   It's been a few years now.

10   Q   What is your position?

11   A   My job doesn't really have a title. And I pretty much do

12   what I am told. But mostly I run the control desk.

13   Q   Would you explain that?

14   A   Gibraltar stores huge amounts of records, a lot of them

15   for doctors. Sometimes doctors need to check out old

16   records, or they need to send new sets of records into

17   storage. All that gets coordinated at the control desk.

18   Calls come in, records come in, tickets get written up,

19   records get pulled, records get sent out. The control

20   desk is the nerve center of the operation.

21   Q   Do you know Dr. Christal Plano?

22   A   Yes. She is a customer. She stores her old patient

23   files with Gibraltar. She also happens to be my sister.

[Document page 39]

1   Q   She helped you get your job with Gibraltar, right?

2   A   Right.

3   Q   What kind of influence does she have with Gibraltar that

4   she could get you a job? You had just gotten out of

5   prison, hadn't you?

6   A   Yeah, but she helped me with the highest influence.

7   Q   What's that?

8   A   Her husband owns the company. Or at least he is one of

9   the owners.

10   Q   So you owe her and her husband a lot of gratitude?

11   A   Sure.

12   Q   On March 15th of this year, she called you and said she

13   needed some help, right?

14   MR. MANNING: I'm sorry to interrupt, but I must object to

15   the leading form of Ms. Ford's questions.

16   THE COURT: Are you objecting to the pending question?

17   MR. MANNING: Yes, Your Honor.

18   THE COURT: Leading is allowed for preliminary questions on

19   direct. The objection is overruled. Ms. Ford, I trust that

20   you will pay attention to the form of your questions as you

21   get into the heart of the matter.

22   MS. FORD: Certainly, Your Honor.

23   BY MS. FORD:

[Document page 40]

1   Q   Did you have a conversation with Dr. Plano on March

2   15th, YR-00?

3   A   Yes.

4   Q   Would you please relate the conversation?

5   MR. MANNING: If any of this is to be offered for the truth,

6   I object on grounds of hearsay.

7   MS. FORD: It's all offered for the effect on the hearer and

8   as operative facts.

9   THE COURT: If you have a problem with any particular

10   testimony, raise your objection then. Continue.

11   BY MS. FORD:

12   Q   Would you go ahead and relate your conversation with Dr.

13   Plano, please?

14   A   She called me at work. I was like hi, how you doing? She

15   said, I need you to do me a big favor. I went, what's

16   the favor? She's like, you remember that woman cop who

17   shot the guy a few years back? Officer Mary Jo Coburn.

18   Well, I need you to get her file. She was my patient

19   and her file is over there. I need you to pull it. And

20   I'm like, what do you want me to do with it once I have

21   it? And she then went into about how there are cassette

22   tapes and she wanted me to pull all the cassettes that

23   were dated in September YR-04. I'm supposed to take

[Document page 41]

1 those tapes home and make copies of them and then

2 replace the originals in the file and put the file back

3 where it belonged.

4 Q Did she tell you what to do with the copies?

5 A Yeah, I am to call this Wally Martinez and tell him I

6 have some very interesting tapes about Mary Jo Coburn

7 and see if he's interested.

8 Q Did Dr. Plano say anything more?

9 A Well, she said that this Coburn lady was trying to get

10 back into police work and it would be some sort of a

11 disaster if that ever happened, and if I could get Mr.

12 Martinez to listen to those tapes it would be all over

13 for Ms. Coburn trying to be a cop again.

14 Q Did she tell you, or did you know, what the tapes were

15 about?

16 A Well, she's a psychiatrist. I figured it was

17 psychiatrist stuff.

18 Q Did she tell you the tapes were confidential?

19 A Not directly. But all the medical records that we store

20 are confidential records. It's a no-brainer to figure

21 that if we've got it it's probably confidential.

22 Q Did she say anything else?

23 A Not really. That's about it.

[Document page 42]

1   Q   What, if anything, did you do as a result of your

2   telephone call with Dr. Plano?

3   A   Well, I did exactly what she asked me to do. I found

4   the tapes, took them home, made copies, replaced the

5   originals, and then called Mr. Martinez.

6   Q   By telephone?

7   A   Yes.

8   Q   How did you get his phone number?

9   A   It's in the phone book. I looked it up.

10   Q   And did you then have a conversation with Mr. Martinez?

11   A   I had several conversations with Mr. Martinez.

12   Q   On what date was your first conversation with him?

13   A   It was about March 18th, 17th, 18th, something like

14   that.

15   Q   You called him?

16   A   Yes.

17   Q   What conversation did you have?

18   A   Well, I said that he didn't know me but I knew he was a

19   reporter and I thought I had some information that he

20   would be interested in. He said, what was it? And I

21   said, it concerns Mary Jo Coburn. He said, really? He

22   was interested. So we arranged to meet.

23   Q   Did you tell him the nature of the information?

[Document page 43]

1   A   I don't recall other than I said he would find it very

2   interesting.

3   Q   Did you tell him the source of the information?

4   A   Not at that time.

5   Q   Was anything else said in that conversation other than

6   what you have related?

7   A   That's about it.

8   Q   Did you and Mr. Martinez subsequently meet?

9   A   Yes.

10 Q   When?

11 A   It took a while for us to get together. When we finally

12   did get together it was on March 23rd.

13 Q   Where did you get together with him?

14 A   It was a restaurant, sort of a café kind of place, near

15   the newspaper office right here in the city.

16 Q   Would you please relate your conversation?

17 A   Well, we more or less went back and forth. He asked

18   what I had. I said I had some tape recordings involving

19   Mary Jo Coburn. He asked what was on the tapes and I

20   said I did not know exactly, but I did know that they

21   involved Ms. Coburn talking to her psychiatrist. I

22   figured they probably had something to do with the

23   shooting. He asked me what I wanted for them. It had

[Document page 44]

1   not occurred to me to ask for money. But I don't like

2   to pass up an opportunity, so I told him the tapes would

3   cost him $2,000. He didn't seem bothered by that. But

4   he kept asking me, how will I know that these tapes are

5   really Mary Jo Coburn and not some other gal talking to

6   her shrink. We went back and forth about that and I

7   started to think that maybe he wasn't really interested

8   in the tapes. Or maybe the price put him off. So I told

9   him that if he wanted to make sure these tapes were the

10   real McCoy he should call Dr. Plano and ask her. I had

11   made a very short taped copy of the very beginning of

12   one of the tapes, and I said, here, play this for her

13   and see what she says. And I guess that's what he did,

14   because he came back a few days later with the $2,000,

15   and he bought the tapes. And that's all I know.

16   Q   When did he actually buy the tapes from you?

17   A   He called me on March 29th and said he had talked with

18   Dr. Plano on the phone and he definitely wanted the

19   tapes and we tried to work out when we could get

20   together. Actually, we didn't get together again until

21   almost a week later, when I gave him the tapes and he

22   paid me $2,000.

23   Q   Do you recall what the date was when you exchanged the

[Document page 45]

1   tapes for the $2,000?

2   A   It was the 2nd of April.

3   Q   Do you know how Mr. Martinez got Dr. Plano's number?

4   A   Sure. I gave it to him.

5   Q   Are you sure that you told him that these tapes were of

6   psychiatric or psychotherapy sessions?

7   A   Words to that effect, yes.

8   Q   Did you tell him they were confidential?

9   A   Well, that seems sort of obvious. I don't remember

10   whether I used those words.

11   Q   Did you tell him that Dr. Plano wanted to see the tapes

12   publicized?

13   A   Yes.

14   Q   Did you tell him why Dr. Plano wanted the tapes

15   publicized?

16   A   I told him she thought Coburn was a rogue cop and she

17   wanted to keep her from getting a police job.

18   Q   Where did you get that from?

19   A   That's what she told me.

20   Q   Did Dr. Plano tell you that she wanted to stay in the

21   background so that she could maintain deniability of any

22   responsibility for leaking the tapes?

23   A   Yeah, something like that.

[Document page 46]

1   Q   But you didn't follow her directions on that, did you?

2   A   Well, I did at first. But pretty soon I realized that

3   there was going to be no sale unless I told Mr. Martinez

4   the whole story. He was just very suspicious about the

5   whole deal. So I felt I had to level with him if I was

6   going to make the sale, so that's what I did.

7   Q   What exactly do you mean by level with him?

8   A   I mean tell him where I got the tapes from and what they

9   were about and why Dr. Plano wanted him to publish them.

10 MS. FORD: That's all the questions I have for now.

11 THE COURT: Cross-examination?

12 CROSS-EXAMINATION BY MR. MANNING:

13 Q   Mr. Klepperman, your sister did you a huge favor in

14   helping you get your job?

15 A   Yes, sir.

16 Q   You were having a hard time finding employment because

17   you had just gotten out of prison, correct?

18 A   That's right.

19 Q   What were you in prison for?

20 A   A burglary and some other stuff.

21 Q   As a matter of fact, you were convicted in YR-08 of four

22   counts of lewd and lascivious conduct, two counts of

23   burglary, and one count of sexual battery?

[Document page 47]

1   A   That's right.

2   Q   Those were all felonies?

3   A   I guess so.

4   Q   And you were sentenced to a total of eight years, right?

5   A   Yes, but I got out three years early because of good

6   behavior.

7   Q   With a record like that, you had a hard time getting a

8   job, didn't you?

9   A   Are you kidding? Of course I did.

10 Q   Your sister helped you out by prevailing on her husband

11   to give you a break?

12 A   I guess that's the way it was.

13 Q   You owe her and her husband a great deal, don't you?

14 A   I do.

15 Q   You would be willing to do a lot in return to help her

16   out if she ever needed it, right?

17 A   Absolutely.

18 Q   Do you realize your sister is in a lot of trouble for

19   letting these tapes leak out?

20 A   I know she is sorry she did it. What kind of trouble is

21   she in?

22 Q   Did you know she could be sued for a lot of money for

23   what she did?

[Document page 48]

1 A Well, I never really thought about it, but that makes

2   sense to me.

3 Q Did you know that if she can shove the blame off on Mr.

4   Martinez then she might come out of the lawsuit a lot

5   better off?

6 A No.

7 Q Does it occur to you that by saying that Mr. Martinez

8   was really in on the deal as far as knowing what was

9   going on, it makes Mr. Martinez's involvement appear to

10   be much stronger and thus might help get your sister off

11   the hook?

12 A Well, I suppose the thought may have crossed my mind

13   like, hey, whose ox is going to be gored if I get up

14   there and tell the truth about what happened and how

15   those tapes got loose?

16 Q Have you talked with your sister about your having to

17   come to court and testify today?

18 A No. We don't get together very often.

19 Q Have you ever gone over with her what you should say if

20   you were called as a witness?

21 A No.

22 Q But you have been told, have you not, that if Mr.

23   Martinez can distance himself from Dr. Plano, then Dr.

1   Plano will be the one who is left holding the bag?

2   A   Yes.

3   Q   Who told you that?

4   A   Ms. Ford.

5   MR. MANNING: Thank you, Mr. Klepperman. You may stand down.

6   MS. FORD: Wait a minute. I have a redirect.

7   REDIRECT EXAMINATION BY MS. FORD:

8   Q   Mr. Klepperman, how did it happen that you and I had a

9   conversation?

10   A   You called and said you wanted to interview me and go

11   over what my testimony might be.

12   Q   Did I volunteer information about what might happen to

13-   your sister, or did you dig that out of me?

14   A   I asked you and you answered. I think you laid out a

15   number of different possibilities.

16   Q   Did I ever tell you what I wanted you to say in your

17   testimony?

18   A   Yes.

19   Q   What did I tell you?

20   A   You said you just wanted me to tell the truth and I

21   should not be worried about the effect of my testimony.

22   MS. FORD: Nothing further.

23   THE COURT: Mr. Manning.

[Document page 50]

1   MR. MANNING: No further questions.

2   THE COURT: Thank you for your testimony, Mr. Klepperman.

3   You may be excused. Do you have another witness, Ms. Ford?

4   MS. FORD: Plaintiff will call two more witnesses. They

5   should be quite brief. Our next witness is Joseph Ball.

6   TESTIMONY OF JOSEPH BALL

7   WITNESS SWORN

8   DIRECT EXAMINATION BY MS. FORD:

9   Q   Good morning. Your name is Joseph Ball spelled B-A-L-L.

10   Is that correct?

11 A   Yes, ma'am.

12 Q   It's Inspector Ball, correct?

13 A   That's correct.

14 Q   Inspector Ball, what is your occupation?

15 A   I am a sworn peace officer. I have worked for several

16   different law enforcement agencies at the federal,

17   state, and local levels. For the past eight years, I

18   have worked for the Dewey City Police Department. I was

19   a lateral hire at the level of captain. Four years ago I

20   was promoted to the rank of inspector, which is the

21   highest rank below the chief of police. On that

22   occasion, I was named to head the internal affairs

23   division, which has been my position up to the present

[Document page 51]

1   time.

2   Q   What is the internal affairs division?

3   A   We are the police who police the police. We are like a

4   separate and independent police department within the

5   overall department. We investigate all allegations and

6   suspicions of police misconduct at any level within the

7   department. When our investigations uncover criminal

8   violations by police officers, we present the results of

9   our investigations directly to the District Attorney.

10   If we uncover violations of departmental regulations, we

11   communicate our recommendations directly to the chief of

12   police. We also work closely with the training division

13   because often our investigations indicate improvements

14   that could be made in the training of our officers.

15   Q   Are you familiar with an internal affairs investigation

16   of the shooting of Ubumu Victoire by Officer Mary Jo

17   Coburn in YR-06?

18   A   I am aware that there was such an investigation, but it

19   was before my time.

20   Q   Are you aware of any allegations that that investigation

21   was a whitewash and that police wrongdoing was covered

22   up?

23   A   I have heard speculation to that effect but I don't know

[Document page 52]

1   of any hard evidence to prove it or even enough to

2   launch an official investigation. We don't take action

3   on the basis of rumors.

4   Q   Are you aware in a general way of the individual

5   officials and officers within the Dewey City Police

6   Department who might have been implicated in such a

7   scheme? Did the speculations seem to point to

8   particular officers or groups of officers that you could

9   identify if asked?

10 A   Yes. I am aware in a general way of the particular

11   officers who were the subjects of this speculation and

12   of the higher police officials who would necessarily

13   have been involved if there had been such a thing as a

14   cover-up.

15 Q   Are those individuals still employed by the Dewey City

16   Police Department?

17 A   For the most part, no. All of the higher officials to

18   whom speculation might have pointed fingers or who would

19   have had to have been involved if there was a cover-up

20   have retired except for one, and that one is on long-

21   term disability leave and is not expected to return to

22   active duty. There were several line officers who were

23   involved in one way or another in the shooting — not the

[Document page 53]

1   shooting but the events surrounding the shooting.   In

2   particular the arresting officers who were involved in

3   the decision to arrest Mr. Victoire and then turn him

4   over to Officer Coburn.   Two of those were found guilty

5   of violating departmental rules and were reprimanded.

6   Neither of them is still with our department.   Two out

7   of the other three arresting officers have since left

8   the Dewey City Department.   One left police work

9   altogether. I think he went to mortuary school.   The

10   other transferred to a different agency.   The one who

11   remains has since been promoted up the ranks to

12   lieutenant.   As a matter of fact, that officer is my

13   deputy, that is to say, he is second in command in the

14   internal affairs division.

15 Q   You are aware that Ms. Coburn has brought this lawsuit

16   to prevent audiotapes of her psychotherapy sessions with

17   a psychiatrist from being published on the Internet and

18   in other places?

19 A   Yes, I am generally familiar with this litigation.

20 Q   Does the Dewey City Police Department have any interest

21   in learning what Ms. Coburn said to her psychiatrist?

22 A   Not that I can think of.   Police officers are among the

23   top occupations that utilize counseling and psychiatric

[Document page 54]

1   services. Police work is stressful, and many police

2   officers encounter times when counseling is needed to

3   help them deal with work-related stresses or stresses on

4   the marriage or family. Psychiatric counseling depends

5   on confidentiality. You have to trust your counselor or

6   your psychiatrist before you can even begin to have a

7   therapeutic relationship. I would say if the police

8   department has any interest in those tapes, it is an

9   interest in their confidentiality being preserved

10   inviolate.

11   Q   If those tapes should reveal information about laxity of

12   police procedures that were involved in the Victoire

13   shooting, would your division have any interest in that

14   information?

15   A   Very little. It is old news. Our department's firearms

16   procedures and arrest and custody procedures have all

17   been thoroughly reviewed and revamped since YR-06.

18   Whatever happened in YR-06, the conditions giving rise

19   to it no longer exist.

20   MS. FORD: No further questions.

21   CROSS-EXAMINATION BY MR. MANNING:

22   Q   What is the statute of limitations for murder in this

23   state?

[Document page 55]

1   A   There is none. Murder can be prosecuted at any time, no

2   matter how much time has passed.

3   Q   If those tapes contain evidence that Ms. Coburn murdered

4   Mr. Victoire, they could be the basis for a successful

5   murder prosecution, couldn't they?

6   A   I am not really competent to answer that question. You

7   would have to ask the District Attorney. Of course, the

8   intuitive answer to your question is yes. But I am not

9   sure what the empirical answer is.

10 Q   If I as a member of the bar of this state with

11   considerable prosecutorial experience were to put it to

12   you that those tapes might contain admissible evidence

13   of a murder, would you be in any position to take issue

14   with my statement?

15 A   Mr. Manning, taking issue with a statement of yours

16   would be one of the last things I would want to do if I

17   valued my peace of mind.

18 Q   Thank you for the compliment, but I wonder if you would

19   be so kind as to answer the question?

20 A   If those tapes contain admissible evidence of a murder,

21   I assume that they could be used in court to help

22   convict the murderer.

23 MR. MANNING: Thank you, Inspector Ball.

[Document page 56]

1   MS. FORD: Just one or two more questions, if Your Honor

2   please.

3   REDIRECT EXAMINATION BY MS. FORD:

4   Q   Inspector, do you have any information as to what is on

5   those tapes?

6   A   I do not.

7   Q   You testified on direct about the importance of

8   psychiatric counseling for maintaining the mental health

9   of police officers and about the indispensable role of

10   confidentiality in that process. On cross-examination

11   you essentially denied that there is some theoretical

12   public interest in what police officers tell their

13   psychotherapists. Putting those two themes together,

14   would you please tell the court and counsel if a police

15   officer went to a psychiatrist and told her psychiatrist

16   in confidence that she had committed a crime, could that

17   information be used against that officer in a court of

18   law?

19   A   Not usually. The privilege for confidential

20   communications between doctor and patient and between

21   psychotherapist and patient would prevent that

22   information from being used in court unless the

23   privilege were to be waived. And, of course, if a

[Document page 57]

1   patient is presently dangerous, the doctor may have an

2   obligation to warn possible victims of the patient's

3   violent tendencies. But that is another matter.

4   MS. FORD: Thank you, Your Honor. We have no more questions

5   of this witness.

6   MR. MANNING: No questions.

7   THE COURT: Thank you, Inspector. You are excused. Counsel,

8   the court has two brief matters that must be disposed of

9   immediately after the lunch hour. Could you be back at

10   1:30?

11   BOTH COUNSEL: Yes, Your Honor.

12   THE COURT: Very well. We will stand in recess until 1:30

13   this afternoon.

14   (COURT IN RECESS FROM 12:05 P.M. TO 1:42 P.M.)

15   THE COURT: Back on the record in Coburn versus Martinez. I

16   apologize for the delay. Ms. Ford, did you have another

17   witness?

18   MS. FORD: Yes, Your Honor. Plaintiff calls Armando

19   Dominguez.

20   TESTIMONY OF ARMANDO DOMINGUEZ

21   DIRECT EXAMINATION BY MS. FORD:

22   Q   Good afternoon, sir. Would you please state and spell

23   your name for the record.

1   A   Yes. My name is Armando Dominguez. That's spelled A-R-

2   M-A-N-D-O D-O-M-I-N-G-U-E-Z.

3   Q   Thanks. Now, Mr. Dominquez, where do you live?

4   A   In New Taft, Tennessee.

5   Q   What kind of work do you do?

6   A   I am a sergeant in the police department of New Taft. I

7   am assigned to the human resources unit. My principal

8   responsibilities have to do with personnel, in

9   particular the recruitment and retention of young men

10   and women who want to get into police work with the New

11   Taft Department.

12   Q   What are you here for today?

13   A   You originally brought this case to my attention, Ms.

14   Ford. Mary Jo Coburn is an applicant for a police patrol

15   job with the New Taft Police Department. You asked me to

16   come to court and testify about the status of her

17   application.

18   Q   What is its status?

19   A   Her application has survived first-stage review, which

20   means basically that all the forms are filled out

21   correctly and all the documentation appears to be

22   complete and in order. Her application is now at

23   second-stage review, which means we are in the process

[Document page 59]

1   of verifying data and checking references. It was in

2   anticipation of that stage of review that Ms. Coburn was

3   advised of the desirability to submit additional

4   documentation about the YR-06 shooting incident. In

5   addition, since she had a history of psychiatric

6   treatment, she was advised to get a letter from her

7   psychiatrist. This is not a strict requirement. It is

8   considered along with all the other relevant information

9   in determining whether an applicant should be moved to

10   third-stage review. A few days ago, Ms. Coburn asked

11   that her application be placed on hold in the middle of

12   the second stage. If and when she asks to have her

13   application reactivated, it will be a very simple

14   process. At the third stage, we would make our own

15   efforts to determine an applicant's actual fitness. For

16   instance, a copy of the report of your latest physical

17   examination with your private physician may satisfy the

18   physical requirements for the second stage, but in the

19   third stage we will have an applicant examined by a

20   doctor of our choice to determine whether the applicant

21   meets the physical fitness requirements. Since Ms.

22   Coburn has a history of psychiatric treatment, she would

23   almost certainly be examined by a doctor, a psychiatrist

[Document page 60]

1   or a psychologist working on contract with our

2   department, in order to make an assessment of her

3   fitness for police work at this point in time from the

4   mental and emotional standpoint.

5   Q   How do you weed out applicants who have a tendency for

6   violence?

7   A   That will come out in work history and psychological

8   testing.

9   Q   Would a tape of a psychotherapy session between an

10   applicant and her psychiatrist some six years earlier be

11   considered by your department in determining an

12   applicant's fitness to be hired?

13   A   Most of us would be quite uncomfortable using that as a

14   source of information. Insofar as it is generally

15   privileged against disclosure, the issue has not arisen.

16   Q   Sergeant Dominguez, let us assume for purposes of the

17   next few questions that the tapes of Ms. Coburn's

18   psychotherapy sessions have relevant and useful

19   information as to whether she has a tendency to

20   violence. Would that be relevant to her eligibility to

21   be hired by your department?

22   A   Of course. There is no place for violence-prone

23   individuals in police work.

1   Q   So, if you were aware of the existence of such a tape,

2   might you ask an applicant to waive confidentiality in

3   order to make the information available to your office?

4   A   Theoretically, yes, we could do that. As a practical

5   matter, we would probably honor the original

6   confidentiality and not go prying into it. On the other

7   hand, the existence of such information would at least

8   suggest a higher degree of scrutiny when we conduct our

9   own mental fitness inquiry. There are no fixed rules.

10   But where there is a question, we try to seek reliable

11   answers using our own resources.

12   Q   Now I would like you to assume a situation in which you

13   are aware of psychiatric records that would be relevant

14   to your assessment of the emotional fitness of an

15   applicant for police work. Assuming that you have it

16   within your power to ask the applicant to waive

17   confidentiality, would there be any significant

18   enhancement of your decision making if you were to

19   require that the psychiatric records be exposed to the

20   public at large?

21   A   I don't see how that would help. More likely it would

22   be counterproductive.

23   Q   From your viewpoint as a person who may have to be

[Document page 62]

1   involved in assessing Ms. Coburn's fitness for police

2   work, would your decision-making process be enhanced by

3   having the tapes of her psychiatric sessions in

4   September YR-04 posted on the World Wide Web?

5   A   No.

6   MS. FORD: Your witness.

7   MR. MANNING: No questions.

8   MS. FORD: Plaintiff rests.

9   THE COURT: Mr. Manning, how many witnesses do you expect to

10   call?

11   MR. MANNING: Just one, Your Honor.

12   THE COURT: You may proceed.

13   MR. MANNING: Call the defendant, Wally Martinez.

14   TESTIMONY OF WALLY MARTINEZ

15   WITNESS SWORN

16   DIRECT EXAMINATION BY MR. MANNING:

17   Q   Mr. Martinez, would you please introduce yourself to the

18   court?

19   A   Certainly. Good afternoon, Your Honor. I am Wally

20   Martinez. My last name is spelled M-A-R-T-I-N-E-Z. As

21   you know, I am a journalist. I am 34 years old. I live

22   here in Dewey City with my wife and three children. I

23   am a YR-09 graduate of the New York University School of

[Document page 63]

1   Journalism and Communications. I have been a journalist

2   all my life. I even put out a little neighborhood

3   newspaper when I was a kid. I was editor of my high

4   school newspaper. That paper won top honors in the state

5   competition the year I was editor. I worked as a

6   stringer for various newspapers and radio and TV

7   stations while I was in college. In YR-07 I was hired

8   as a staff writer for the Dewey City Herald. In YR-02 I

9   refocused my career on Internet journalism through my

10   Web site, which is known as outlaw cops dot com. I still

11   take on occasional newspaper and magazine assignments,

12   but most of my time goes into the Web site.

13   Q   Tell us about outlaw cops dot com.

14   A   This is a serious journalistic site that specializes in

15   stories and issues regarding law enforcement, in

16   particular issues of police shootings, questionable

17   arrests, brutality, all kinds of inappropriate behavior.

18   Q   Do you have a vendetta against the police?

19   A   Not at all. I really admire most police officers. They

20   perform a huge public service and receive inadequate

21   recognition and compensation. They also wield

22   tremendous power in our society, especially over

23   powerless people such as the poor, people of color,

[Document page 64]

1   political dissidents, and the like. My Web site focuses

2   on exposing police abuses so that the entire law

3   enforcement community can be purged of the bad apples

4   and enjoy the respect and prestige that it generally

5   deserves.

6   Q   How is your Web site set up? What would I find if I

7   went there on my computer?

8   A   The home page contains a mission statement, some brief

9   vignettes of exemplary cases of police misconduct, and

10   links to other Web sites with similar interests, such as

11   Amnesty International. The heart of the Web site is in

12   a series of links to so-called case studies, in which

13   there is detailed information about particular cases

14   that I have investigated or that have come to my

15   attention. In the case studies there are newspaper

16   articles, witness interviews, photographs, and

17   multimedia presentations. For the most part it is

18   strictly factual, but there are also editorial pieces in

19   which I reflect on the significance of various cases.

20   My Web site also has a bulletin board section where

21   visitors can post comments or whatever. Sometimes I

22   learn about new cases from comments posted on the

23   bulletin board. Sometimes there can be pretty lively

[Document page 65]

1   discussions on the bulletin board. There is a small

2   segment of users who are pro police all the way and

3   think the police can do no wrong. They post some pretty

4   provocative messages sometimes. The rest of the

5   regulars have a more realistic view. Does that answer

6   your question?

7 Q Yes, indeed. Now how did you come to be interested in

8   the subject of police abuses?

9 A Well, as a matter of fact it started with this very

10   case. In YR-06 when Mr. Victoire was killed, I was

11   assigned to cover the story for the Herald. I followed

12   the investigation, court proceedings, and the like. I

13   wrote a series of articles that focused on the question

14   of whether Officer Coburn's action was justified.

15 Q What were your impressions of this case?

16 A Well, I never could figure out how it could be called a

17   case of justifiable homicide. She shot him in the back.

18   She claimed he was coming at her and that she had to

19   kill him to save her own life, but the physical evidence

20   contradicts her claim. Beyond that, there are some very

21   interesting questions about how he came to be arrested,

22   why he was then turned over to a single unaccompanied

23   police officer who was a rookie and who happened to be

[Document page 66]

1   on the small side. Mr. Victoire was a big man, and he

2   had just engaged several male officers in quite a

3   struggle to subdue him. At least that is what they

4   claimed. It made no sense that they would let Officer

5   Coburn take him to the emergency room all alone. And

6   then when she removed his handcuffs in the ER, that to

7   my mind was so incredibly reckless I couldn't believe

8   it. Very little in the case made sense except the

9   reality of an unarmed man who had been shot and killed

10   by a cop. The other thing was that the so-called

11   investigations that led to her being exonerated were

12   conducted in secret and have never been released to

13   public view. They remain as classified documents so we

14   have no idea what these investigations consisted of.

15   And then of course there was the amazing turn of events

16   when the wrongful death suit by Mr. Victoire's family

17   against Ms. Coburn went through several days of

18   testimony and then all of a sudden there is a settlement

19   and everyone goes home. What was that settlement? Why

20   did it happen? Nobody knows because the parties to that

21   lawsuit took an oath of silence. As far as I'm

22   concerned there must have been some dramatic development

23   and Ms. Coburn and whoever was backing her paid a

[Document page 67]

1   handsome sum to buy the silence of all the other

2   players.

3   Q   You say whoever was backing her. What do you mean?

4   A   Well, I don't have any hard evidence. But it seems to

5   me quite unlikely that she was in this all alone.

6   Q   There are a lot of questions about this case that were

7   never resolved?

8   A   You bet. And I think the public has a right to know

9   exactly what happened in this case. Here's an apparent

10   setup for what might have been a murder and a hidden

11   process by which the whole thing gets whitewashed.

12   That's outrageous in my opinion.

13 Q   Where do the tapes fit in?

14 A   Well, the tapes contain statements made by Ms. Coburn

15   around the same time of the civil trial and on the eve

16   of the secret settlement.

17 MS. FORD: Your Honor, plaintiff objects to any reference to

18 the contents of the tapes. You have already ruled in our

19 pretrial conference that they are privileged communications.

20 I move to strike the last question and answer and ask that

21 the witness and counsel be admonished.

22 THE COURT: The identity of the voices on the tapes and the

23 dates when they were made are not confidential and may be

[Document page 68]

1   referred to. Anything actually said on the tapes is

2   privileged. The court agrees that the last question and

3   answer came rather close to the forbidden area, but they did

4   not cross the line. Objection overruled. But please be

5   very careful, Mr. Manning.

6   MR. MANNING: Yes, sir.

7   BY MR. MANNING:

8   Q   You were relating how you came to be interested in

9   police abuses and you described how you were assigned to

10   cover the Victoire killing and your impressions of that

11   case. Were there other things that influenced your

12   career track in this direction?

13 A   As I became more and more involved in this case I

14   researched other similar cases to see whether this case

15   departed from the norm. While there are countless

16   police shootings, I found very few where the post-

17   shooting response by the police departments was as

18   closed as this one. At least in modern times. But my

19   investigations into other cases produced a gold mine of

20   information that I thought to be of enormous public

21   interest. I wasn't going to write a book about them, so

22   I decided to set up the outlaw cops dot com Web site.

23 Q   Why no book?

[Document page 69]

1   A   What's interesting about these cases is the constantly

2   changing nature of the information that comes out.

3   Witnesses come forward, witnesses change their stories,

4   connections between seemingly unrelated incidents become

5   visible. A book is cast in stone. My Web site can track

6   constantly changing developments, new cases, and the

7   like.

8   Q   Is there a Victoire and Coburn section on your Web site?

9   A   There used to be, but the case seemed to be pretty much

10   closed after YR-02 or so. I pulled it down after a

11   while because other cases were so much more important

12   and interesting.

13   Q   How did you come into possession of the tapes?

14   A   I received a telephone call from Forrest Klepperman

15   sometime last March.

16   Q   Do you remember the date?

17   A   May I look at my notes?

18   THE COURT: Would your notes help you refresh your

19   recollection?

20   THE WITNESS: I think so.

21   THE COURT: Go ahead.

22   BY MR. MANNING:

23   Q   Do you remember now?

[Document page 70]

1   A   Yes, the phone call came in on March 18.

2   Q   Did you know Mr. Klepperman?

3   A   I had received a few tips from him in the past. So I

4   recognized his voice and I knew that generally speaking

5   the information he passed on was reliable.

6   Q   What kinds of information had he given you in the past?

7   A   Well, I really don't want to get into the details, if

8   you don't mind. That Mr. Klepperman has been a source of

9   mine in the past is OK with both me and Mr. Klepperman

10   to come out, but the details might compromise other

11   sources and so as a journalist I have to make a judgment

12   to protect those sources.

13 Q   I will withdraw the question. By the way, is your

14   telephone number listed in the phone book?

15 A   No, it is unlisted.

16 Q   How long has it been since you had a number listed in

17   the telephone book?

18 A   At least five years.

19 Q   Do you know how Mr. Klepperman got your number?

20 A   He has had it for some time now. I gave it to him. When

21   he first started giving me news tips I wanted him to be

22   able to reach me.

23 MR. MANNING: Your Honor, I have here a Dewey City phone book

[Document page 71]

1   for YR-00. I have already shown this to Ms. Ford. I call

2   the court's attention to page 203, where there are over a

3   hundred listings for people named Martinez, but there is no

4   listing for a Wally Martinez. I would ask the court to take

5   judicial notice of that fact.

6   THE COURT: Any objection?

7   MS. FORD: No objection.

8   THE COURT: Very well, judicial notice will be taken as

9   requested.

10   BY MR. MANNING:

11   Q   Mr. Martinez, would you please recount your conversation

12   with Mr. Klepperman on March 18?

13   A   After we greeted each other and exchanged a few

14   pleasantries he asked if I remembered the Mary Jo Coburn

15   case. I said I certainly did. Well, he said, I have

16   some very hot information for you. What is it? It's a

17   couple of cassette tapes that you will find very

18   interesting. What's on them? He told me in some detail

19   but I don't think I should get into that. But it

20   definitely piqued my interest. We arranged to get

21   together. Then he told me he wanted $2,000 for the tapes

22   and I said nothing doing unless I could independently

23   authenticate the tapes and verify that the information

[Document page 72]

1   was as significant as he claimed. I didn't want to have

2   a libel suit on my hands, and if this was some sort of

3   imposter or something I could get in real trouble if I

4   was not careful. So we arranged to meet on March 23 and

5   he let me listen to parts of the tapes, which confirmed

6   to me that the information was new and extremely

7   important. But he did not let me have the tapes at that

8   point or make copies or anything. But he did provide me

9   with a brief excerpt from one of the tapes that I could

10   use if I wanted to try to ascertain that the voices on

11   the tape were Mary Jo Coburn and her psychiatrist.

12 Q So you knew the tapes were of one or more psychiatric

13   counseling sessions?

14 A Mr. Klepperman had referred to the shrink, and the style

15   and manner of the conversations definitely sounded like

16   my idea of psychotherapy. I had a bit of psychotherapy

17   myself a while back after a crisis following a death in

18   my family, and the style of conversation seemed pretty

19   much the same as what that was like.

20 Q Did Mr. Klepperman mention the name of Dr. Plano?

21 A No.

22 Q Did he tell you that Ms. Coburn had applied for a police

23   job in Tennessee?

[Document page 73]

1 A I don't believe so. I learned about that later on.

2 Q Who from?

3 A Ms. Coburn.

4 Q Did he tell you anything about the psychiatrist being

5   concerned to stop Ms. Coburn from getting a police job

6   and wanting these tapes publicized in order to put the

7   kibosh on Ms. Coburn's plans?

8 A Nothing like that. All he said was that the tapes were

9   of Ms. Coburn and a shrink, as he called it, and that

10   they contained statements by Ms. Coburn that I would be

11   interested in. That's all.

12 Q Did he tell you how he had come into possession of the

13   tapes?

14 A No, he didn't tell, and I didn't ask.

15 Q Why not?

16 A Sometimes you're better off not to know these things. I

17   trust my sources and I do not want to have any more

18   information about their procedures than they want to

19   volunteer to me. Mr. Klepperman did not volunteer.

20 Q What efforts if any did you make to verify that the

21   tapes were genuine?

22 A I called Ms. Coburn.

23 Q How did you know how to get hold of her?

[Document page 74]

1   A   I didn't at first. But I searched the Internet for her

2   name, which led to the Web site for the school where she

3   works in Tennessee. I got a phone number from the

4   school. And so I called her.

5   Q   When did you call her?

6   A   April 3rd.

7   Q   What was said in your conversation with her?

8   A   I introduced myself and told her why I was calling.

9   Q   Did you recognize her voice?

10   A   Oh, yes. She has a very twangy voice. I was pretty sure

11   it was her on the tape. And I know it was her on the

12   phone.

13   Q   You had heard her voice before?

14   A   Many times.

15   Q   So after you told her why you were calling, how did she

16   react?

17   A   She acted dumbfounded. She wanted to know why I was

18   calling her after so much time. At first I said it was

19   just a routine follow-up. We talked for a while and

20   then I said that I wanted to play a tape for her to see

21   if she could recognize the voices, and she said OK. So

22   I played the little excerpt that Mr. Klepperman had

23   provided me, and she said that's me, all right. And she

[Document page 75]

1   immediately wanted to know where I got that tape and how

2   much more did I have and what did I intend to do with

3   them. When I told her what I had and what I intended to

4   do, she became very upset with me. It was like she

5   would do anything to stop me. Well, I had the

6   verification I needed and so I wasn't much interested in

7   talking about not publishing the tapes at that point. In

8   fact in between my phone calls with Ms. Coburn I called

9   Mr. Klepperman and told him that I was prepared to buy

10   the tapes at his asking price.

11   Q   Did you have more than one telephone call with Ms.

12   Coburn?

13   A   Yes, I think we had three or four conversations.

14   Q   On what dates?

15   A   It was over two or three days in the first week of

16   April. I don't remember the exact dates.

17   Q   Why such extensive communication if you had gotten the

18   information you needed?

19   A   When Ms. Coburn realized my intentions, she said that

20   she could provide me with much more interesting

21   information than the tapes. She claimed to have

22   documents that would fully expose the investigations

23   following the Victoire shooting. She hinted at a police

1   cover-up and perhaps a larger pattern of police

2   corruption against which her little case would fade into

3   insignificance. Naturally, I was interested. But she

4   would only pass the information on to me if I would give

5   her the tapes and promise not to publish them. It took

6   several conversations for us to thrash all that out,

7   because we were both being extremely cautious. We had to

8   establish trust. In the end, I finally came to the

9   conclusion that she did not have any documents, or at

10   least any useful documents. I decided her whole thing

11   about documents was a ruse to try to talk me out of the

12   tapes. At that point I cut off negotiations with her.

13   The next thing I know I am being slapped with temporary

14   restraining orders from two different courts, and now I

15   am embroiled in this lawsuit.

16 Q Did you receive the tapes from Mr. Klepperman?

17 A Yes, before I had actually finished my conversations

18   with Ms. Coburn, I had a meeting with Mr. Klepperman

19   where I paid him $2,000 and he delivered the tapes.

20   They consisted of two cassettes with three sides of

21   program material. One side is blank.

22 Q Did you listen to the tapes in their entirety?

23 A Yes.

[Document page 77]

1   Q   Have you let anyone else listen to them?

2   A   No.

3   Q   Have you revealed the contents of the tapes to anyone

4   else other than perhaps your legal counsel?

5   A   No.

6   Q   Is it your intention to upload those tapes onto your Web

7   site?

8   A   Yes, at least substantial portions of them. There are

9   some parts that are not particularly newsworthy that I

10   would not intend to use. But I definitely want to

11   upload the newsworthy parts. I want to create a case

12   study page with a retrospective on the Victoire shooting

13   and follow-up and then use the tapes as newly revealed

14   information.

15   Q   You speak of "newsworthy." You heard the testimony that

16   practically everyone in the Dewey City Police Department

17   who had anything to do with this case is now gone and

18   that those tapes won't be of much interest to the police

19   officials in New Taft, Tennessee, where Ms. Coburn has

20   applied for a police job. Does that testimony affect

21   your judgment as to the newsworthiness of the tapes?

22   A   Absolutely not. In the first place, I know that several

23   of the guys who were involved in the Victoire

[Document page 78]

1   investigation are still on the police force here in

2   Dewey City or are in the district attorney's office.

3   Second of all, it doesn't matter. The newsworthiness of

4   the tapes does not depend on who is still around and who

5   has retired and all that. This was an interesting,

6   conflicted, and dramatic story a few years back, and any

7   new information that puts a new twist on that story or

8   delivers new information would be highly newsworthy. And

9   the police department needs to be exposed to its own

10   history, whether or not the individuals who were

11   involved are still there. If an institution does not

12   understand its own history, it may be doomed to repeat

13   it. From the readership viewpoint, police shootings are

14   a hot topic. This is definitely a high public interest

15   piece.

16 Q   Even though it concerns events that occurred several

17   years ago?

18 A   Absolutely. How long ago did the Titanic go down? How

19   long ago did Amelia Earhart disappear? Yet every time

20   some new scrap of information comes up about those cases

21   it's front-page news. I'm not saying this is the

22   Titanic, but it was definitely big news here in Dewey

23   City and these tapes will be big news too, believe me.

[Document page 79]

1   Q   Where are the tapes now?

2   A   They are in a safe deposit box. That's where the TRO

3   told me to put them. They are safe. No one but me has

4   access to them.

5   Q   Now, Mr. Martinez, just to be clear, did you ever have

6   any contact with Dr. Plano about these tapes?

7   A   I have never had any contact with Dr. Plano about

8   anything.

9   Q   No telephone calls or telephone conversations?

10   A   None.

11   Q   Did you have any reason to believe that Dr. Plano was

12   behind these tapes being leaked to you?

13   A   Not at all. The first time I ever heard such an idea

14   was when I heard her testify this morning.

15   Q   When you bought these tapes, was part of your purpose to

16   help Dr. Plano carry out her plan?

17   A   Of course not. I never heard of her plan, assuming it

18   existed.

19   Q   Mr. Klepperman testified that he told you all about Dr.

20   Plano and actually put you in touch with Dr. Plano.

21   A   That's dead wrong. Nothing like that happened.

22   Q   Will you receive any benefit from publishing these

23   tapes?

[Document page 80]

1   A   Personally, no. There's nothing in it for me. The

2   tapes are newsworthy and I operate an outstanding

3   journalistic Web site. The most I'll get is the

4   satisfaction of uncovering the truth. The big benefit

5   from publishing these tapes will be to the people of

6   Dewey City, New York, who may gain new insight into a

7   notorious homicide case and new information about police

8   administration in this city, and the people of

9   Tennessee, who will have new information about the kind

10   of people who are being considered for police work in

11   that state and will have a better basis for evaluating

12   the quality of police administration in that state.

13   MR. MANNING: Thank you, Mr. Martinez. Your witness.

14   CROSS-EXAMINATION BY MS. FORD:

15   Q   Have you read Ms. Coburn's complaint in this action?

16   A   Yes.

17   Q   Have you read her declaration in support of the motion

18   for a TRO?

19   A   Yes.

20   Q   Did you read the parts about the extreme emotional

21   distress that she has suffered as a result of your

22   actions?

23   A   Yes.

1 Q Do you have any reason to doubt the truthfulness of

2   those statements?

3 A I have no idea what's in her mind.

4 Q You knew at the time you first considered publicizing

5   her medical records that it would be distressing to her,

6   didn't you?

7 A Not really.

8 Q Did you think she would take pleasure in having her

9   deepest secrets publicized to the whole world?

10 A Of course not.

11 Q Did you even stop to think about how she would react?

12 A I figured she wouldn't be overjoyed, but that's not

13   relevant to my responsibilities as a journalist.

14 Q As a matter of fact, you realized full well that this

15   would be emotionally devastating to her, didn't you?

16 A Well, of course, but that's not my responsibility. She

17   has to take responsibility for her own actions.

18 Q About your Web site, how do you finance it?

19 A Advertising.

20 Q Do you make a profit?

21 A A little bit. A thousand or so a month.

22 Q Does your profitability depend on the popularity of your

23   site?

[Document page 82]

1   A   The advertising rates for a Web site are based on the

2   average number of hits it receives.

3   Q   You would fully expect that the publication of Ms.

4   Coburn's confidential tapes of her psychotherapy

5   sessions would draw in a large number of additional

6   hits, wouldn't you?

7   A   I imagine so. It's a big story.

8   Q   So, in addition to serving the public interest as you

9   see it and enhancing your reputation as a journalist,

10   publication of these tapes would benefit you

11   financially, right?

12   A   Maybe a little bit. Not much.

13   Q   Do you have any estimate of how much more money you will

14   be able to make from advertising on your Web site if you

15   are allowed to publish Ms. Coburn's confidential

16   communications with her psychiatrist?

17   A   No, I don't.

18   MS. FORD: No further questions.

19   MR. MANNING: No redirect, Your Honor. The defense rests.

20   THE COURT: Does plaintiff wish to present any evidence in

21   rebuttal?

22   MS. FORD: No, Your Honor.

23   THE COURT: Then the matter is submitted. I am not going to

1   ask you for oral argument at this time. It's too late in the

2   day. Perhaps later. The court will need to study the

3   transcript of today's testimony before it can rule. Is there

4   anything further? If not, the court will stand in recess.

5   (COURT RECESSED AT 3:15 P.M.)

Ford & Burns
Phelps Building
233 Dodge Street
Dewey City, New York 13213
Telephone: (891) 776-5400

> UNITED STATES DISTRICT COURT
> **FILED**
> JULY 1, YR-00
> CENTRAL DISTRICT OF NEW YORK

   Elizabeth Ford
   Attorney for Plaintiff,
   Mary Jo Coburn

Manning & Kobalewski
3875 Trupers Pike, Suite 211
Dewey City, New York 13213
Telephone (891) 777-6563

   Dean Manning
   Attorney for Defendant,
   Wally Martinez

In the
UNITED STATES DISTRICT COURT
FOR THE CENTRAL DISTRICT OF NEW YORK

MARY JO COBURN)	
)	
Plaintiff)	
)	Civil Action No. 00-386 JDS
vs.)	
)	Judge: John Dell Small, Jr.
WALLY MARTINEZ)	
)	
Defendant)	

STIPULATION RE FINAL HEARING AND JUDGMENT

On June 27, YR-00, the court held an evidentiary hearing on plaintiff's motion for

a preliminary injunction. On June 29, YR-00, the court, through its clerk, inquired of

[Document page 1]

counsel whether either party would object to treating the hearing on plaintiff's motion for a preliminary injunction as the final hearing on the merits of plaintiff's claim for a permanent injunction and, if so, how the court should proceed on plaintiff's prayer for damages. In response to the court's inquiry, the parties, through undersigned counsel, have conferred and agreed, and hereby stipulate as follows:

1. Both parties having had a full and fair opportunity to offer all relevant evidence at the hearing on plaintiff's motion for a preliminary injunction, neither party objects to the court treating that hearing as the final hearing on the merits of plaintiff's claim for a permanent injunction, pursuant to Fed.R.Civ.P. 65(a)(2).

2. If the court finds for the plaintiff and enters a permanent injunction, the court should simultaneously enter a final judgment on plaintiff's claim for damages and should award the plaintiff nominal damages, plus her costs.

3. If the court finds for the defendant on the grounds that plaintiff is not entitled to a permanent injunction even though plaintiff has made out a valid cause of action against the defendant for damages, the court should enter a final judgment, pursuant to Fed.R.Civ.P. 54(b), dismissing plaintiff's claim for a permanent injunction, should allow the parties a period of 45 days within which to complete discovery on the issue of damages, and should thereafter place plaintiff's claim for damages on the trial calendar, with costs to abide the outcome.

[Document page 2]

4. If the court finds for the defendant on the grounds that plaintiff has not made out a cause of action against the defendant for either injunctive relief or damages, the parties agree that the court should enter a final judgment dismissing the complaint and awarding defendant his costs.

5. If the court enters a judgment under either paragraph 3 or paragraph 4 of this stipulation, plaintiff reserves the right to seek an injunction pending appeal.

Dated: July 1, YR-00

Respectfully submitted,

Elizabeth Ford
Elizabeth Ford

Ford & Burns
Phelps Building
233 Dodge Street
Dewey City, New York 13213
Telephone: (891) 776-5400

Attorney for Plaintiff,
Mary Jo Coburn

Dean Manning
Dean Manning

Manning & Kobalewski
3875 Trupers Pike, Suite 211
Dewey City, New York 13213
Telephone (891) 777-6563

Attorney for Defendant,
Wally Martinez

[Document page 3]